Apple Pro Training Series

Motion 4
Quick-Reference
Guide

Brendan Boykin and Jem Schofield

Apple
Certified

Apple Pro Training Series: Motion 4 Quick-Reference Guide
Brendan Boykin and Jem Schofield
Copyright © 2011 Jem Schofield and Brendan Boykin

Published by Peachpit Press. For information on Peachpit Press books, contact:

Peachpit Press
1249 Eighth Street
Berkeley, CA 94710
(510) 524-2178
www.peachpit.com
To report errors, please send a note to errata@peachpit.com.
Peachpit Press is a division of Pearson Education.

Apple Series Editor: Lisa McClain
Project Editor: Nancy Peterson
Development Editor: Bob Lindstrom
Production Coordinator: Cory Borman
Technical Editor: Charles Meyer
Copy Editor: Darren Meiss
Proofreaders: Dan Foster, Susan Festa
Compositor: James D. Kramer, Happenstance Type-O-Rama
Indexer: Jack Lewis
Cover Illustrator: Kent Oberheu
Cover Producer: Chris Gillespie

ISBN 13: 978-0-321-63677-5 ISBN 10: 0-321-63677-5
9 8 7 6 5 4 3 2 1 Printed and bound in the United States of America

Contents at a Glance

Chapter 1	Motion Basics	1
Chapter 2	Text	23
Chapter 3	Shapes, Masks, and Paint	35
Chapter 4	Particles and Replicators	49
Chapter 5	Timelines	67
Chapter 6	Keyframes	77
Chapter 7	Behaviors	87
Chapter 8	Filters	97
Chapter 9	Cameras and Views	105
Chapter 10	Manipulating Objects in 3D	113
Chapter 11	Lights, Shadows, and Reflections	119
Chapter 12	Working with Other Applications	125
Chapter 13	Exporting	135
Appendix	Keyboard Shortcuts	139

Table of Contents

Chapter 1   Motion Basics. 1

Utility Window 2
Canvas Window 6
Toolbar. 10
Project Pane (F5) 13
Timing Pane (F6) 17
Heads-Up Display (F7). 19
Setting Project Properties and Preferences. 19

Chapter 2   Text 23

Creating Text. 23
Modifying Text in the Inspector Tab. 24
Modifying Text in the HUD. 29
Using the Adjust Glyph Tool 29
Using Text Generators 30
Working with Text Behaviors. 32

Chapter 3   Shapes, Masks, and Paint 35

Creating Simple Shapes 35
Creating Custom Shapes 36
Modifying a Closed Shape 38
Creating Masks 40
Modifying Masks. 41
Adding an Image Mask. 41

Using the Paint Stroke Tool 43
Modifying a Paint Stroke 44
Modifying the Control Points of
    a Shape, Mask, or Paint Stroke. 45
Using Shape Behaviors 46

Chapter 4   **Particles and Replicators**. **49**
Particle System 49
Replicators. 57

Chapter 5   **Timelines** **67**
Working in the Mini-Timeline 67
Working in the Timeline 71
Working with Markers 76

Chapter 6   **Keyframes**. **77**
Setting Keyframes Manually .77
Using Record Animation to Create Keyframes 79
Using the Keyframe Editor. 80
Modifying Keyframes in the Timeline 85
Converting Behaviors to Keyframes 86

Chapter 7   **Behaviors** **87**
Applying Behaviors. 87
Modifying Behaviors. 89
Example Behaviors 90
Applying Parameter Behaviors 92
Modifying Parameter Behaviors 93
Example Parameter Behaviors. 93

Chapter 8   Filters 97
Applying Filters. 98
Modifying Filters. 99
Example Filters 102

Chapter 9   Cameras and Views 105
Adding a Camera 105
Modifying a Camera. 106
Positioning a Camera 107
Camera Behaviors. 110
Views 110

Chapter 10   Manipulating Objects in 3D. 113
2D Layering vs. 3D Positioning. 113
Using the 3D Transform Tool in the Canvas 114
Using the 3D Transform Tool in the HUD. 116
3D Behaviors. 117

Chapter 11   Lights, Shadows, and Reflections 119
Adding a Light. 119
Adjusting Lighting Parameters 120
Disabling Lighting. 121
Activating and Adjusting Shadows 122
Disabling Shadows 122
Activating and Adjusting Reflections 123

Chapter 12   Working with Other Applications 125
Roundtripping with Final Cut Pro 125
Using Motion Templates in Final Cut Pro 130
Working with Adobe Photoshop Documents 131
Working with Adobe Illustrator Documents 132

Chapter 13   Exporting 135
Using File > Export. 135
Using File > Share. 138

Appendix   Keyboard Shortcuts 139
Interface 139
View Tools 142
Create Tools. 143
Mask Tools. 144
Camera and Effects Icons. .145
Canvas 145
Timing 146
Project 147

Index. 149

1
Motion Basics

Motion 4 allows you to create simple text graphics or complex animations for your visual projects (documentaries, features, news, digital signage, and so on). With an easy-to-learn interface and rich tool set, Motion is your in-house special effects solution.

The incredible compositing power of Motion is organized into two main windows: the Canvas and Utility windows. Each of these windows is composed of multiple panes in which your project creation and modification is performed. Motion also has a built-in dashboard window, the Heads-Up Display (HUD), that provides quick access to often modified parameters.

Utility window   Canvas window

Utility Window

The Utility window has three main tabs: the File Browser, Library, and Inspector. In these tabs—which can be detached to create additional instances of the Utility window—you can import custom objects, add preset objects to your project, and transform those objects.

File Browser (Command-1)

Motion's File Browser allows you to import objects into projects. It is directly linked to your system's Finder.

Preview area
Display a visual preview (with playback when applicable) and information about the selected object.

Import button
Add the selected object to your project (centering the object in the Canvas when applicable).

Sidebar
Navigate to connected volumes/network locations. Find a desired object by clicking an item or using the navigational buttons/search field.

File stack
Display the contents of the location selected in the Sidebar. Drag an object from this area to the Canvas or click the Import button at the top of the Utility window to add the object to your project.

New folder
Click to create a new folder at the selected location.

Show image sequences as collapsed
Collapse sequentially numbered images into a single object. Allows importing an image sequence as a single movie object.

TIP ▸ The Sidebar and Stack perform like a Finder window. You can create a new folder and reorganize, rename, or delete files.

NOTE ▸ When importing an object, Motion does not copy/collect the object's file; it simply references the file at its current location.

Library (Command-2)

The Library provides access to all of the royalty-free content, behaviors, filters, generators, particle emitters, and replicators installed with Motion. It also contains shapes, shape styles, gradients, and text styles; and offers quick access to your iTunes and iPhoto libraries.

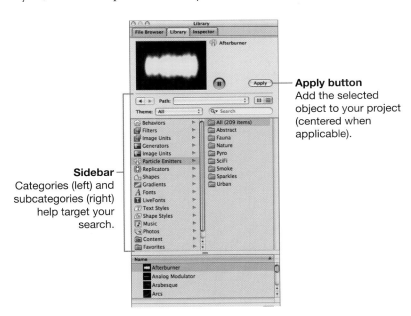

Apply button
Add the selected object to your project (centered when applicable).

Sidebar
Categories (left) and subcategories (right) help target your search.

TIP ▶ When you install Motion, the default location for the Library content is Users/Username/Library/Application Support/Motion. The Library content is available to use in any Motion project.

Inspector (Command-3)

The Inspector tab includes every control to transform an object (which becomes a layer when placed inside your project), group, effect, camera, or light. The Inspector comprises four subtabs: Properties, Behaviors, Filters, and Object.

NOTE ▶ The fourth tab, Object, is a utility tab that changes its name based on the selected object type (Shape, Image, and so on).

Properties (F1)

The Properties tab in the Inspector contains all of the core prop-
erty parameters of a selected object. In this tab, you can transform
a selection, change its blend mode, and tweak parameters related to
lighting, shadows, and timing. You can also apply keyframes and
parameter behaviors to most settings.

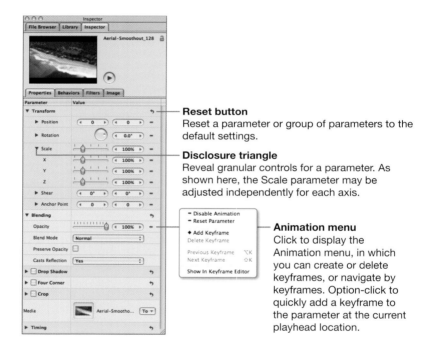

Reset button
Reset a parameter or group of parameters to the
default settings.

Disclosure triangle
Reveal granular controls for a parameter. As
shown here, the Scale parameter may be
adjusted independently for each axis.

Animation menu
Click to display the
Animation menu, in which
you can create or delete
keyframes, or navigate by
keyframes. Option-click to
quickly add a keyframe to
the parameter at the current
playhead location.

NOTE ▶ The parameters list changes appearance based on the
currently selected object type.

Behaviors (F2)

Behaviors are Motion's tool for animating objects without setting
keyframes. When you add behaviors to selected objects in your project, they are listed in the Behaviors tab.

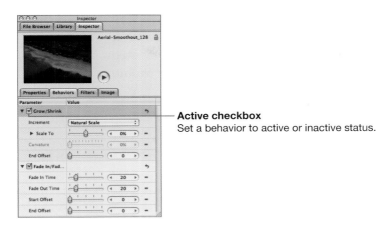

Active checkbox
Set a behavior to active or inactive status.

Filters (F3)

Filters allow you to achieve distinctive looks. As you add filters to selected objects, their parameters are listed in the Filters tab.

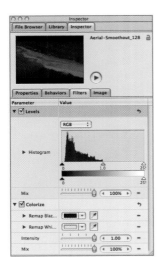

TIP Filter order can affect the visual results of your project. Drag a filter name to a higher or lower position in the list to change the order in which filters are applied.

Object (F4)

The Object tab label changes depending on the currently selected object type. For example, if you select an image object, the tab will be labeled Image; if you select a text object, the tab will be labeled Text. The tab's properties also reflect your selection.

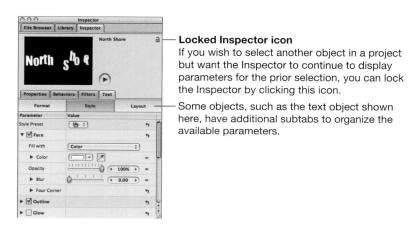

Locked Inspector icon
If you wish to select another object in a project but want the Inspector to continue to display parameters for the prior selection, you can lock the Inspector by clicking this icon.

Some objects, such as the text object shown here, have additional subtabs to organize the available parameters.

Canvas Window

The Canvas window is your main workspace. Here you build your project and create your composition. This composing process is done by direct manipulation of the Canvas workspace and in conjunction with the Inspector tab and the HUD. Two panes in the Canvas window are not visible when your start a new project: Project and Timing.

Canvas

The Canvas is the most prominent area of the Canvas window and acts as your composition area. You can transform objects, aim lights, and draw shapes in addition to performing many other tasks. The look and performance of the Canvas is dependent on the other areas of the Canvas window.

Project pane

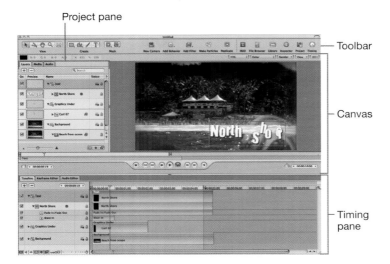

Toolbar

Canvas

Timing pane

With an object selected in the Canvas, you can use a number of tools to directly manipulate that object. You can also Control-click (or right-click) an object to access the Object shortcut menu to access even more options.

Status bar

View options

Canvas

Mini-Timeline

Scale handle
Shift-dragging the object handle will scale an object
proportionately. Shift-Option-dragging an object will
scale it proportionately from its center.

Rotation handle
Shift-drag the rotation
handle to rotate the
object in 45-degree
increments.

Anchor point
Centered on an object by default.
Left justified on text by default.

Status Bar

The Status Bar displays information about your project. You can
choose which of three options are displayed in the Appearance pane
of Motion > Preferences (refer to "Setting Project Properties and
Preferences" in this chapter).

Color
View the pixel information
for the pointer location.

Coordinates
View the location
of the pointer.

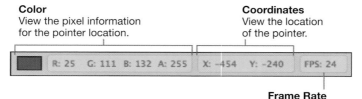

Frame Rate
See the current frame rate in frames per second
(fps). Visible only during project playback.

View Options

Here you can customize the Canvas's appearance. These controls not
only affect the project's onscreen display, but they also influence the
project output format during export.

NOTE ▶ You can override these settings in the Output tab of the Export window or by using Share commands.

Render
Set the resolution quality and render options. Refer to the following image for more details.

Set the display mode for objects in the Canvas. For better interactivity, choose Draft or Normal when working on a project and change to Best when exporting a project.

Set the resolution of the Canvas. A lower level can improve playback performance.

Access the Advanced Quality options to apply more control over the display mode of objects. See the *Motion User Manual* for more information.

Zoom level
Set the Canvas's zoom level. Pressing Shift-Z will perform a "Fit-to-Window" zoom setting; pressing Option-Z will force the Canvas to 100%.

Toggle render options related to your project.

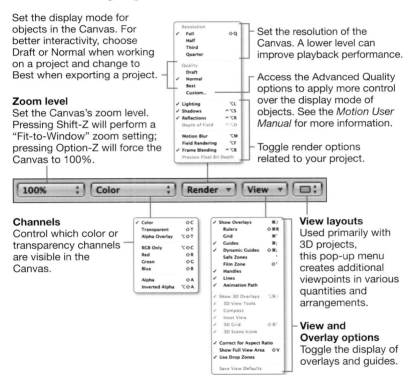

Channels
Control which color or transparency channels are visible in the Canvas.

View layouts
Used primarily with 3D projects, this pop-up menu creates additional viewpoints in various quantities and arrangements.

View and Overlay options
Toggle the display of overlays and guides.

Mini-Timeline

The mini-Timeline provides simple control over project timing and playback. You can trim the duration or adjust the timing of a selected object, which is designated as a clip. More comprehensive timing adjustments are made in the Timing pane (discussed later in this chapter.)

Play Range In Point
(Command-Option-I)
Force playback to
start at this point.

Play Range Out Point
(Command-Option-O)
Force playback to end
at this point.

View the project
duration.

Playhead   Play from start   Loop playback

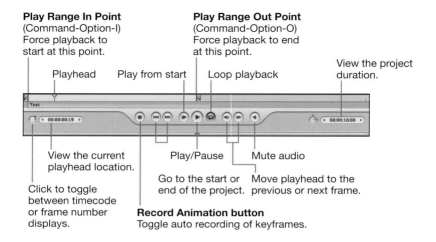

View the current
playhead location.

Click to toggle
between timecode
or frame number
displays.

Play/Pause   Mute audio

Go to the start or   Move playhead to the
end of the project.   previous or next frame.

Record Animation button
Toggle auto recording of keyframes.

TIP Press Option-X to clear the current play range.

Toolbar

In the Motion Toolbar, you can create and edit project objects, add cameras and effects, and show or hide interface elements. You can also customize the Toolbar to provide quick access to favorite tools and often-used parts of the user interface.

Create tools   Camera and Effects buttons   Show/hide the
Toolbar

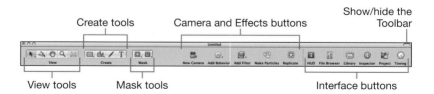

View tools   Mask tools   Interface buttons

View Tools

This section of the Toolbar contains tools to manipulate and adjust objects in the Canvas.

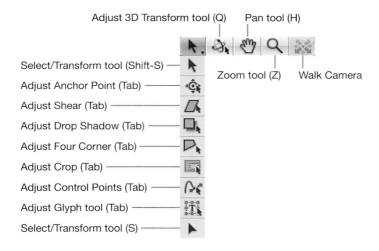

Adjust 3D Transform tool (Q)   Pan tool (H)

Select/Transform tool (Shift-S)
Adjust Anchor Point (Tab)
Adjust Shear (Tab)
Adjust Drop Shadow (Tab)
Adjust Four Corner (Tab)
Adjust Crop (Tab)
Adjust Control Points (Tab)
Adjust Glyph tool (Tab)
Select/Transform tool (S)

Zoom tool (Z)   Walk Camera

NOTE ▶ In addition to using the keyboard-specific shortcuts shown, you can repeatedly press Tab to cycle through the tools under the Select/Transform tool and the Adjust 3D Transform tool, depending on the selected object type.

Create Tools

The Create tools include shape, paint, and text tools. See Chapter 3, "Shapes, Masks, and Paint," for more information on the shape tools. See Chapter 2 for more information on creating text using the Text tool.

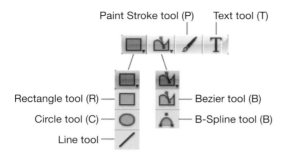

NOTE ▸ Press B to toggle between the Bezier and B-Spline tools.

Mask Tools

Motion includes a variety of Mask tools, including Bezier and B-Spline. See Chapter 3 for more information on Mask tools.

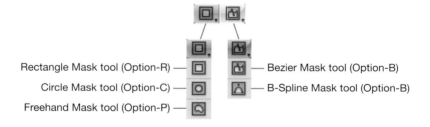

NOTE ▸ Press Option-B to toggle between the Bezier Mask and B-Spline Mask tools.

Camera and Effects Buttons

These buttons allow you to add cameras, behaviors, and filters to your project. You can also create particle systems or replicators from a selected object.

Add a new behavior to the selected layer/group. See Chapter 7.

Create a particle system from the selected layer. See Chapter 4.

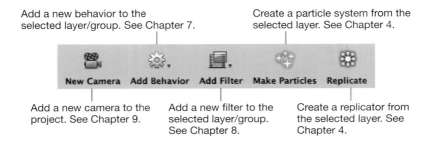

Add a new camera to the project. See Chapter 9.

Add a new filter to the selected layer/group. See Chapter 8.

Create a replicator from the selected layer. See Chapter 4.

Interface Buttons

These buttons give you fast access to most of the user interface.

Show/hide the Utility window with the File Browser tab active (Command-1).

Show/hide the Utility window with the Inspector tab active (Command-3).

Show/hide the Timing pane of the Canvas window (F6).

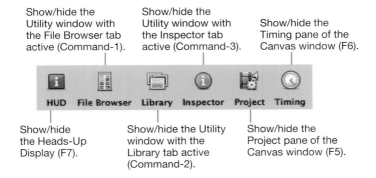

Show/hide the Heads-Up Display (F7).

Show/hide the Utility window with the Library tab active (Command-2).

Show/hide the Project pane of the Canvas window (F5).

Project Pane (F5)

The Project pane is your project organization hub. It contains three tabs: Layers, Media, and Audio.

Layers Tab (Command-4)

Here you can access all of the objects in your project. Every object is represented as a layer. Layers can be consolidated into groups. Those layers and groups can be renamed in the Layers tab.

Groups
Organize layers or other groups for organizational purposes or for effect consolidation. For example, if you wish to move several objects in unison, drag the objects' layers into a group, and then apply one behavior to the group. All of the grouped objects will be affected.

Create or delete a group.

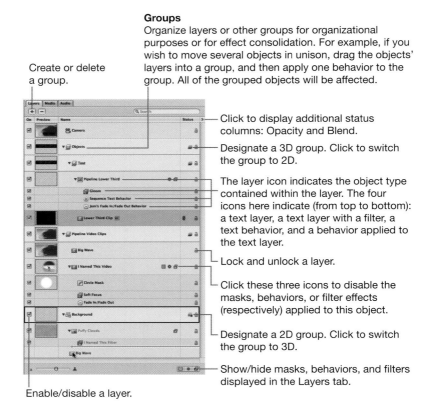

Click to display additional status columns: Opacity and Blend.

Designate a 3D group. Click to switch the group to 2D.

The layer icon indicates the object type contained within the layer. The four icons here indicate (from top to bottom): a text layer, a text layer with a filter, a text behavior, and a behavior applied to the text layer.

Lock and unlock a layer.

Click these three icons to disable the masks, behaviors, or filter effects (respectively) applied to this object.

Designate a 2D group. Click to switch the group to 3D.

Show/hide masks, behaviors, and filters displayed in the Layers tab.

Enable/disable a layer.

When working with a 2D object, a layer's vertical position within the Layers tab determines the associated object's compositing order in the Canvas. Higher layers are placed in the foreground; lower layers are placed in the background. You can drag the layers to reorganize them or to change their compositing order. An insert bar indicates where an object will appear in the Layers list and the group in which the object will reside.

In this example, the text object will be composited behind the shape but will remain in Group 1.

Before	Drag to see the insert bar below and aligned with the Shape layer's icon.	After

In this example, the text object will be composited behind the Shape but will reside in Group 2.

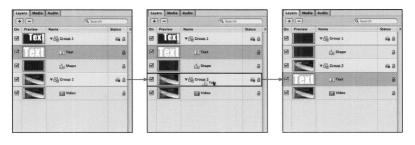

Before	Drag to see the destination group outlined.	After

In this example, the text object will be composited behind the shape and the video while a new group is created to contain the text.

Before	Drag to display the insert bar, and then drag left until the plus sign appears.	After

TIP ▶ You can make duplicate layers by selecting a layer and then Option-dragging the layer within the Layers tab or within the Canvas. Alternatively, you can select a layer and press Command-D.

NOTE ▶ If you have applied a filter or mask to a layer, you may wish to create a Clone layer rather than simply duplicating the layer. Select the layer and then press K to create a clone. Changes made to the filters or masks applied to the original layer will propagate to the same filters and masks present in the clone.

   The rubber stamp icon indicates a clone layer.

Media Tab (Command-5)

The Media tab tracks all outside assets that you have added to your project. These objects—such as QuickTime movies, still images, and audio—are listed along with their media properties such as resolution, pixel aspect ratio, and duration.

Audio Tab (Command-6)

The Audio tab allows you to access the audio files in your project.

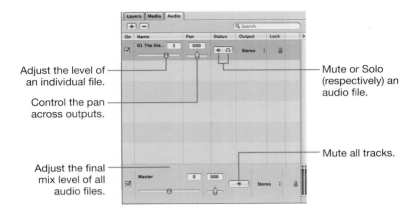

Adjust the level of an individual file.

Control the pan across outputs.

Adjust the final mix level of all audio files.

Mute or Solo (respectively) an audio file.

Mute all tracks.

Timing Pane (F6)

The Timing pane represents your project within time. It includes three tabs: the Timeline, Keyframe Editor, and Audio Editor.

Timeline Tab (Command-7)

While in an application such as After Effects you perform most tasks in the Timeline; in Motion the Timeline is used primarily to make global changes and perform simple project edits.

NOTE ▶ See Chapter 5 for more information on using the Timeline.

Groups and layers are presented as they appear in the Project pane's Layers tab.

Toggle time view, zoom between projects, and play range durations.

Each object is represented as a clip showing the object's timing in relation to the project and other objects.

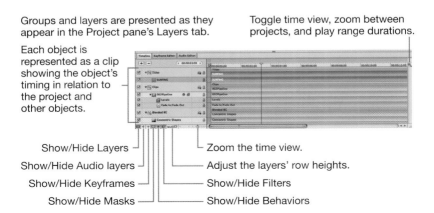

Show/Hide Layers

Show/Hide Audio layers

Show/Hide Keyframes

Show/Hide Masks

Zoom the time view.

Adjust the layers' row heights.

Show/Hide Filters

Show/Hide Behaviors

Keyframe Editor Tab (Command-8)

The Keyframe Editor allows you to work with keyframes in a graph-based environment. Using keyframes, you can animate parameters of filters, behaviors, and objects over time.

NOTE ▶ See Chapter 6 for more information about keyframing.

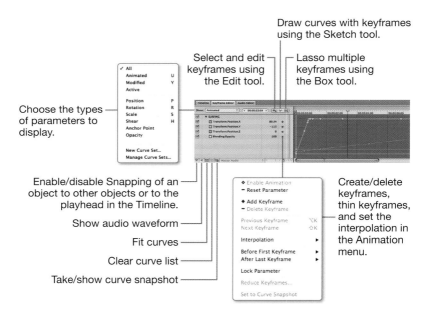

Use the marked audio region for playback.

View the playhead position within the audio track.

Play the audio track.

Jump to start of audio track.

Set the play range.

Enable/disable audio scrubbing when dragging the Audio Editor's playhead.

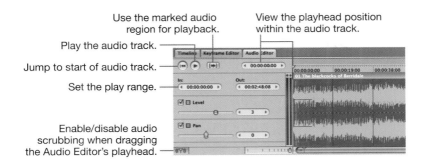

Heads-Up Display (F7)

The Heads-Up Display (HUD) is a floating window that functions like a mini-Inspector. It provides access to the most commonly used parameters. A HUD's appearance changes based on the type of object currently selected.

> **TIP** ▶ You can cycle through HUDs that are attached to an object by pressing D. These HUDs could include filters or behaviors that you applied to a layer as well as properties of the object itself.

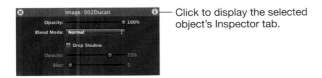

Click to display the selected object's Inspector tab.

Setting Project Properties and Preferences

Beyond the basic interface configuration, Motion allows for customization. Some of these customizations are project-based; others are applied to the application itself.

Project Presets

When starting a new project, you should choose a preset that reflects the frame size and frame rate of your intended output file. The available presets aid you in your choice by featuring the most commonly used codecs. However, these codecs do not determine the output codec. For QuickTime movie output, the default codec is Apple ProRes 4444 (although you can choose another codec if desired).

Click to access all the presets and custom settings to create new projects.

When selected, the Select Project Preset window will no longer appear when you create a new project. The project will be created using the default preset.

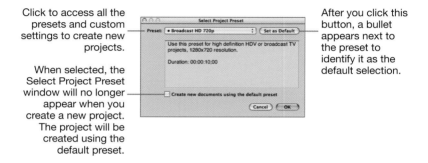

After you click this button, a bullet appears next to the preset to identify it as the default selection.

Project Properties

If necessary, you can alter almost all of your current project's settings by choosing Edit > Project Properties.

Any parameter of a project's properties except the Frame Rate can be changed after it has been created.

The project background color can be set to Transparent, Solid, or Environment.

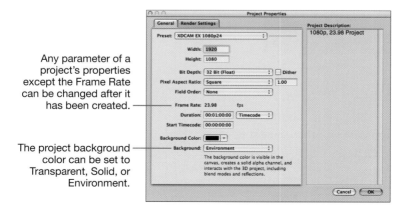

Motion Preferences

Application-wide settings can be accessed by choosing Motion > Preferences. Only a couple of the nine preference panes are shown in the following images.

NOTE ▶ Refer to the *Motion User Manual* for more about Motion Preferences.

Appearance

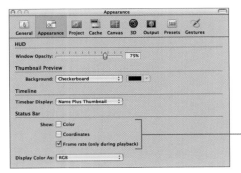

Select the Status Bar Show checkbox to display coordinates and color information based on your pointer's position in the Canvas.

Project

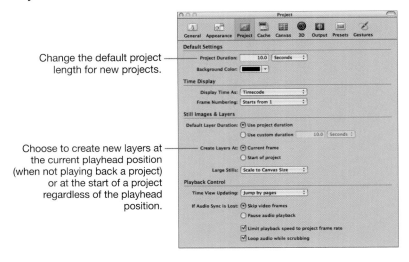

Change the default project length for new projects.

Choose to create new layers at the current playhead position (when not playing back a project) or at the start of a project regardless of the playhead position.

Keyboard Shortcuts

Motion's Command Editor lets you customize the keyboard layout to your liking and save your customized command sets. It is also a great resource for learning Motion keyboard shortcuts.

Whether you want to modify an existing command set or create your own command set from scratch (perhaps to mimic another application such as After Effects), you can customize the keyboard to work the way you want.

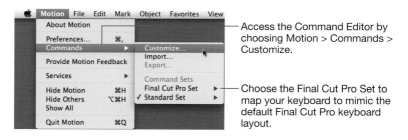

Access the Command Editor by choosing Motion > Commands > Customize.

Choose the Final Cut Pro Set to map your keyboard to mimic the default Final Cut Pro keyboard layout.

Command set options   Modifier key options

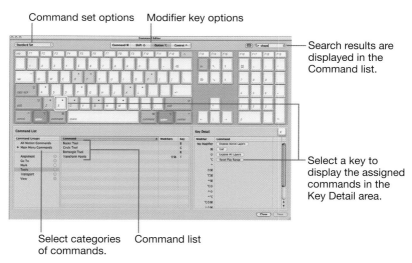

Search results are displayed in the Command list.

Select a key to display the assigned commands in the Key Detail area.

Select categories of commands.   Command list

2
Text

Working with text and titles is a fundamental role of motion graphics. Almost every show opener, lower third, or bumper is embellished with some type of 2D or 3D text. Motion gives you tremendous creative control over how that text is presented and manipulated.

Numerous options are available for creating your text look via the Inspector, the HUD, and the Adjust Glyph tool.

Creating Text

Creating text is one of the simplest functions in Motion. Treat it like word processing: type first, then format.

1   From the toolbar, choose the Text tool.

2   If necessary, select a group in the Layers tab of the Project pane to receive the text element.

3   Click anywhere in the Canvas window.

4   Type your text. You can press Return to start a new line.

5   After entering the text, press the Escape key. A bounding box appears around the text and the Select/Transform tool is chosen.

6   Position your text in the Canvas, as desired.

NOTE ▶ Be sure to press the Escape (or Enter) key to exit text entry mode. To return to text entry mode for additional editing, double-click the text you want to change.

TIP ▶ To display the Title Safe area in the Canvas, choose Safe Zones from the View & Overlay Options pop-up menu.

Modifying Text in the Inspector Tab

Although you have several ways to modify text in Motion, doing so in the Inspector tab provides you with the most control.

1   Select the text you want to modify. You can select an entire text object by choosing the text layer in the Layers tab or by clicking the text in the Canvas. If you want to modify a single glyph or group of glyphs, double-click the text object to highlight all of the glyphs, and then select individual glyphs that you want to modify.

2   In the Utilities window, in the Inspector tab, choose the Text subtab.

There are three panes for text: Format, Style, and Layout.

TIP In addition to making adjustments in the Text tab and its three panes, you can also adjust position and other basic parameters in the Properties subtab.

Format Pane

The Format pane contains parameters to change font families, point size, tracking, kerning, position, scale, and rotation.

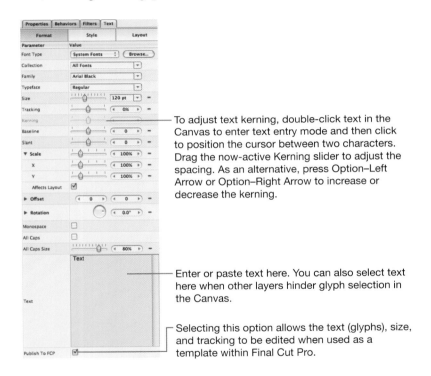

To adjust text kerning, double-click text in the Canvas to enter text entry mode and then click to position the cursor between two characters. Drag the now-active Kerning slider to adjust the spacing. As an alternative, press Option–Left Arrow or Option–Right Arrow to increase or decrease the kerning.

Enter or paste text here. You can also select text here when other layers hinder glyph selection in the Canvas.

Selecting this option allows the text (glyphs), size, and tracking to be edited when used as a template within Final Cut Pro.

Style Pane

In the Style pane, a text object's appearance can be changed using the Face, Outline, Glow, and Drop Shadow options.

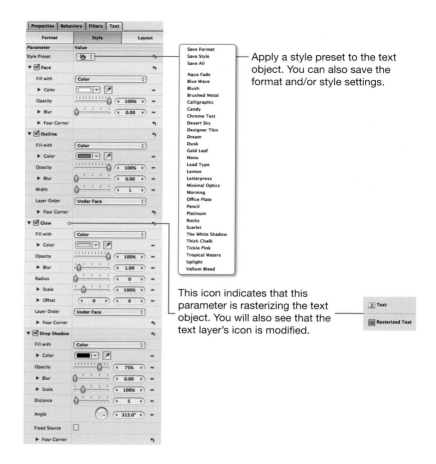

Apply a style preset to the text object. You can also save the format and/or style settings.

This icon indicates that this parameter is rasterizing the text object. You will also see that the text layer's icon is modified.

TIP Almost any parameter in the Inspector can be copied to another object. Simply drag the parameter's name from the Inspector to the object in the Canvas or Layers tab.

Layout Pane

The Layout pane permits complete control of a text object's layout, including the ability to place and animate text on a path, type on text, and modify parameters such as Justification and Line Spacing (leading). You can also choose whether or not the text will face the camera when repositioned in 3D space.

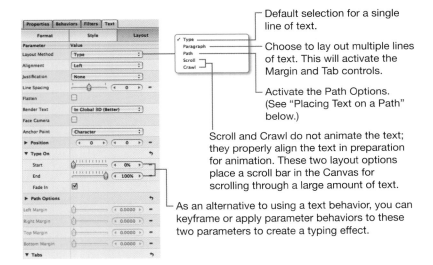

Default selection for a single line of text.

Choose to lay out multiple lines of text. This will activate the Margin and Tab controls.

Activate the Path Options. (See "Placing Text on a Path" below.)

Scroll and Crawl do not animate the text; they properly align the text in preparation for animation. These two layout options place a scroll bar in the Canvas for scrolling through a large amount of text.

As an alternative to using a text behavior, you can keyframe or apply parameter behaviors to these two parameters to create a typing effect.

Placing Text on a Path

You have an almost unlimited number of animation possibilities when placing text on a path. When combined with behaviors or the Record Animation feature (which automatically records keyframes for any changes made to parameters over time), text can travel nearly anywhere.

1   Select a text object.

2   Set the Layout Method to Path.

3   Double-click the text in the Canvas to enter text entry mode.

4   Add, modify, or delete control points in the Canvas.

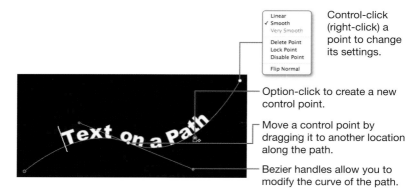

Control-click (right-click) a point to change its settings.

Option-click to create a new control point.

Move a control point by dragging it to another location along the path.

Bezier handles allow you to modify the curve of the path.

5   Change additional parameters in the Path Options group.

Set the starting point of the text on the path.

Allow the text to loop through the start and end control points on the path.

When a Circle path is chosen, for example, the text appears inside, rather than outside, the circle's circumference.

Place the text so that it stays along the created path.

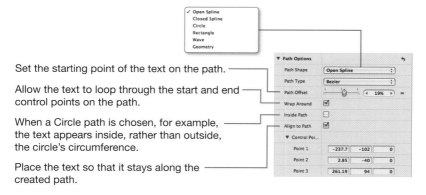

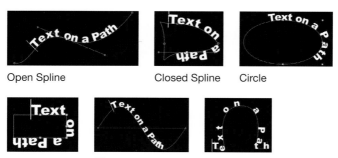

Open Spline   Closed Spline   Circle

Rectangle   Wave   Geometry allows you to create a custom shape, such as those shown here, using the Bezier tools.

Modifying Text in the HUD

The HUD provides quick access to some basic text properties to modify the selected text object or selected glyphs.

Click the font family pop-up menu, and then drag up or down to dynamically choose a font.

Using the Adjust Glyph Tool

The Adjust Glyph tool's Transform Glyph attribute allows you to modify the position and rotation of individual characters in the Canvas.

NOTE ▶ You can also access the Adjust Glyph tool by Control-clicking (right-clicking) a text object in the Canvas and choosing Transform Glyph from the shortcut menu.

When the Adjust Glyph tool is active, the Attribute pop-up menu appears in the Text HUD. It provides control over an individual glyph's position, rotation, face, outline, glow, and drop shadow.

The Adjust Glyph tool works much like the Adjust 3D Transform tool. You can move the glyph along the three axes (green, red, and blue arrows) and rotate around those axes (the three rotation handles, displayed as circles, that illuminate with each axis's respective color).

TIP ▸ Option-click to choose multiple glyphs at once. You can then manipulate them simultaneously using the Transform Glyph attribute.

Using Text Generators

Motion contains four text generators: File, Numbers, Time Date, and Timecode. You'll find the text generators in the Library tab's Generators category.

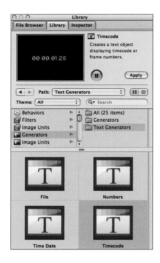

While each generator has unique parameters and applications, all are used to create text that changes information or values over time. The parameters of a text generator are located in a fourth Generator subtab. The following sections show examples of the four generators.

File Generator

Click Browse to select a plain text (.txt) file to be displayed line by line.

Numbers Generator

Select the text formatting from these options.

Time Date Generator

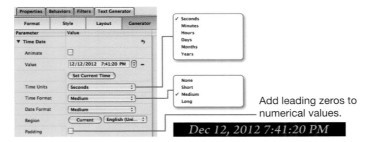

Add leading zeros to numerical values.

Timecode Generator

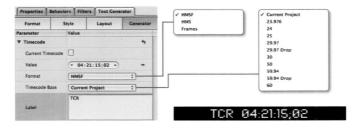

Working with Text Behaviors

Motion's extensive collection of text behaviors can be applied to any text in a project and permits a wide range of ways to animate type.

One such behavior is the Scroll Text behavior. To create simple, scrolling credits, follow these steps:

1 Create or select a text object containing a show or film's credits.

2 From the Toolbar, choose Add Behavior > Text Animation > Scroll Text.

3 Set the Scroll Direction to Vertical. Choosing Horizontal creates crawling text similar to a news ticker.

4 Change the other Scroll Text parameters as desired.

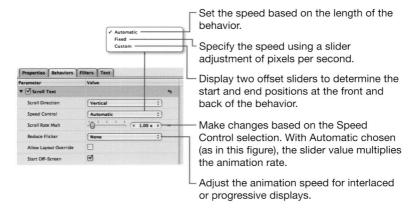

Set the speed based on the length of the behavior.

Specify the speed using a slider adjustment of pixels per second.

Display two offset sliders to determine the start and end positions at the front and back of the behavior.

Make changes based on the Speed Control selection. With Automatic chosen (as in this figure), the slider value multiplies the animation rate.

Adjust the animation speed for interlaced or progressive displays.

NOTE ▸ For more information about applying and modifying behaviors, see Chapter 7, "Behaviors."

The majority of text behaviors were built using the Sequence Text behavior. It is the basis for creating and animating almost any parameter of a text object.

1 Apply the Sequence Text behavior to a text object.

2 From the Parameter Add pop-up menu, choose the parameter you want to animate.

3 Modify the parameter's value to the desired setting.

4 Change the Controls settings as desired.

Animate from the value set in this behavior to the text's value.

In the Add pop-up menu, you can add one or more parameters to a behavior. After a parameter is added, its controls appear at the top of the sequence text. Use the Remove pop-up menu to delete parameters.

Animate from the text's value to the value set in this behavior.

Animate a full cycle starting at the text's value, to the value set in this behavior, and then back to the starting value.

Animate a full cycle starting at the value set in this behavior, moving to the text's value, and then returning to the behavior's value.

Displays the Source parameter with the options to Use Source Animation (use keyframes applied to the source object) or to Ignore Source Animation.

Specify how sequencing progresses within the text object.

Set the behavior's speed to affect each glyph in an object, each object with the animation, or the entire animation.

Complete the animation before starting again from the beginning.

Specify how many glyphs animate simultaneously.

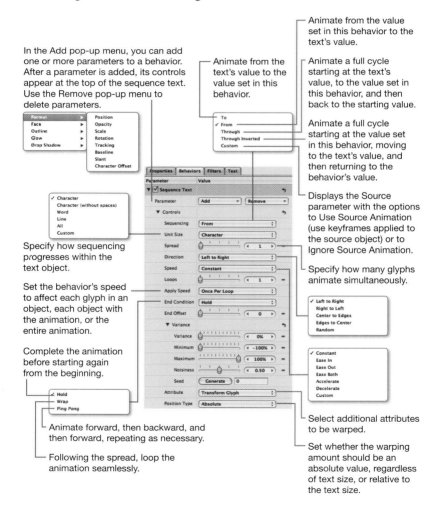

Animate forward, then backward, and then forward, repeating as necessary.

Following the spread, loop the animation seamlessly.

Select additional attributes to be warped.

Set whether the warping amount should be an absolute value, regardless of text size, or relative to the text size.

To fade-in the text glyphs while scaling them down from a larger size, do the following:

1   Choose Add > Format > Scale.

2   Choose Add > Format > Opacity.

3   Change the Opacity value to 0%.

4   Change the Scale value to 300%.

5   If necessary, set Sequencing to From.

6   Adjust the behavior's duration in the mini-Timeline.

Start of behavior ——————————————→ End of behavior

3

Shapes, Masks, and Paint

When creating illustrations, backgrounds, or other design elements, the shape, paint, and mask tools achieve diverse goals: produce filled shapes for use as graphical elements, create elements by using a continuous painting-like movement, and make masks to create transparent areas. Although these three Motion tools perform different functions, they all use control points to create closed or open shapes.

Shapes created with the Bezier tool (left) and the B-Spline tool (right).

A sample of Motion's many brush styles.

A mask used to cut out the rider from one video and drop her over another background.

Creating Simple Shapes

You can create common shapes in Motion using the Rectangle, Circle, and Line tools.

1   From the Toolbar, choose the Rectangle, Circle, or Line tool, depending on which object you want to create.

2   In the Layers tab of the Project pane, select the destination group, if desired.

3   Drag in the Canvas to create the shape.

4   Press Esc to exit the tool.

NOTE ▶ To modify these shapes, see "Modifying the Control Points of a Shape, Mask, or Paint Stroke" in this chapter.

While dragging using the Rectangle tool (left image), the HUD includes very simple controls. After you have created the shape, press Esc (right image) to select the shape object (indicated by the bounding box) to increase the number of HUD settings. As with word processing, you create first and then modify the shape's settings.

TIP ▶ The Rectangle and Circle tools share two features via modifier keys. While dragging with either tool, hold the Shift key to create a symmetrical shape (square versus rectangle or circle versus oval). Also, pressing the Option key during creation will expand the shape from the center out rather than from the insertion point. The Line tool will create straight lines when pressing Shift.

NOTE ▶ Motion includes 16 shape presets—including a quote bubble and a variety of polygons—in the Library tab's Shapes category.

Creating Custom Shapes

The Bezier and B-Spline tools enable more freeform shape creation, helping you create custom shapes with linear edges or smooth curves.

To create a Bezier shape:

1 From the Toolbar, choose the Bezier tool.

2 Click in the Canvas to create a control point.

3 To create additional consecutive control points, you can click to create a single linear point or drag to create a Bezier curve.

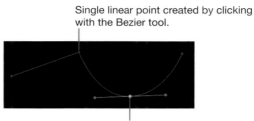

Single linear point created by clicking with the Bezier tool.

Drag the Bezier tool to create a curve with adjustable tangent handles.

TIP ▶ You can adjust a control point's setting by Control-clicking (or right-clicking) the point and choosing an option from the shortcut menu.

The last control point you create determines whether the shape is open or closed.

4 To leave the shape open (outlined only), double-click in the Canvas, or press Return. To close the shape, click the first control point you created, or press C.

NOTE ▶ Press Esc to delete an incomplete Bezier shape.

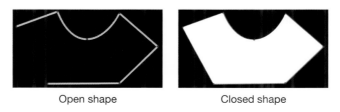

Open shape   Closed shape

When creating a closed shape, the pointer displays a pen point with a circle when the pointer is placed over the first control point.

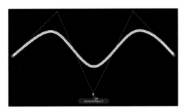

TIP ▶ An open shape becomes a paint stroke—an outlined shape with no fill—which is also what the Line tool creates.

B-Spline shapes differ from Bezier curves because their control points do not lie on the shape. The points are "tractor beams" pulling at portions of the shape, resulting in very smooth curves.

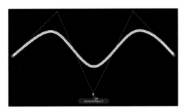

Using the B-Spline tool, only five points were needed to create this sine wave. The last point was double-clicked to create an open shape.

This "amoeba" was also created using the B-Spline tool. The first point was clicked again after creating the other control points, yielding a closed shape.

NOTE ▶ Press Esc to delete an incomplete B-Spline shape.

Modifying a Closed Shape

You can modify closed shapes to change their fill, outline, and geometric parameters. These controls are found in two panes of the Inspector's Shape tab.

Apply a paint brush style for the outline. Fill is disabled.

Choose one of two Fill Modes: Color or Gradient.

Click this third strip to create additional color tags. Modify a tag by selecting it and adjusting the Color parameters.

Choose one of three Brush Types: Solid, Airbrush, or Image. Airbrush and Image can be applied to a paint stroke; choosing one of these two types disables the Fill parameters.

When working with an object with junctions (corners), Joint defines how the outline should fit together: Square, Round, or Bevel.

Define the beginning and end of the outline.

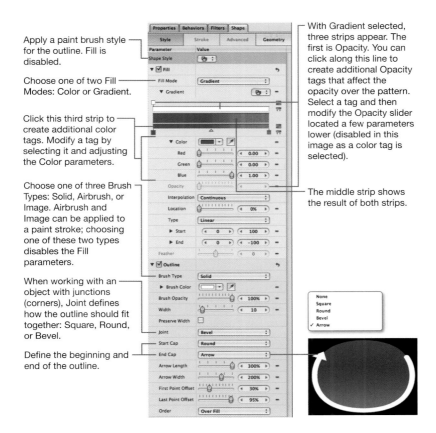

With Gradient selected, three strips appear. The first is Opacity. You can click along this line to create additional Opacity tags that affect the opacity over the pattern. Select a tag and then modify the Opacity slider located a few parameters lower (disabled in this image as a color tag is selected).

The middle strip shows the result of both strips.

NOTE ▶ The Stroke and Advanced tabs apply only to paint strokes.

Choose one of three Shape Types: Linear, Bezier, or B-Spline.

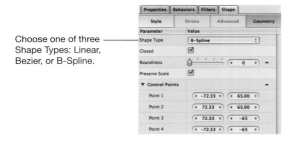

Creating Masks

Mask creation is similar to shape creation. Because masks must be closed shapes, the Line and Paint Stroke tools are not available. However, Motion does provide a Freehand Mask tool—similar to the Paint Stroke tool—that allows you to create masks in a continuous motion.

1   Select the layer or group to be masked.

2   From the Toolbar, choose the desired mask tool.

3   Click in the Canvas to create control points that define the mask's shape.

    ▶   Drag the Rectangle or Circle Mask tool to create a shape. Press Option to expand the mask from the center point; press Shift to expand the mask symmetrically.

    ▶   Use the Freehand Mask tool like a paintbrush. Drag the tool around the Canvas to create the mask shape. Release the mouse button to close the mask.

The Bezier and B-Spline mask tools are similar to their shape counterparts. The exception is that masks must be closed; therefore, the mask will automatically close if you double-click the last point.

Original video ⟶ The Bezier Mask tool was used to cut the rider from the video. ⟶ The masked video is composited over the new background.

NOTE ▶ Mask tools cannot be applied to text layers; however, they can be applied to groups containing text.

Modifying Masks

When you're adjusting masks, the HUD has you covered. To complement the mask control points that you can adjust in the Canvas, the HUD includes all of the parameters necessary to tweak masks.

Switch the solid and transparent portions of the mask

Feather the inside or outside of the mask.

Choose one of four Mask Blend Modes:

Add
Add each new mask to the previously created ones (the default setting).

Subtract
Subtract a mask from the alpha. Great for cutouts.

Replace
Disregard any embedded alpha channel (such as in a TIFF file) and replace it with the new mask.

Intersect
Allow an original object's alpha channel to remain intact and let the new mask intersect with the embedded one.

Adding an Image Mask

Image masks allow any object to define transparency. They are excellent for creating transitions between clips or for creating interactions between the image mask's source object and the target object.

To add an image mask:

1   Select the object to receive the image mask.

2   Choose Object > Add Image Mask.

3   Create or add the object to be used as the mask source for the image mask and trim to where it will start and finish.

4   In the Layers tab, drag the mask source to the Image Mask layer.

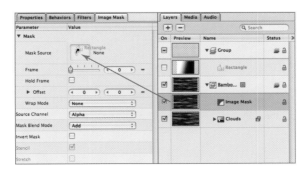

5   Adjust the image mask parameters.

> In the case of this grayscale rectangle, the
> Source Channel was set to Luminance.

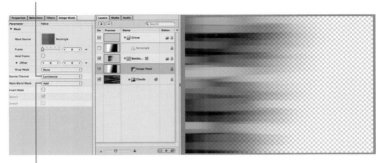

> As with regular masks, this parameter has Add,
> Subtract, Replace, and Intersect settings.

Using the Paint Stroke Tool

Any shape can be converted into a paint stroke by activating the
shape's Outline parameters and deactivating its Fill parameters.
However, when you wish to create a paintbrush effect using a continuous movement in the Canvas, you should use the Paint Stroke tool.

1   From the Toolbar, choose the Paint Stroke tool.

2   In the Layers tab, select the destination group.

3   In the Canvas, drag the pointer to create a brush stroke.

4   Press Esc to exit the tool and select the paint stroke.

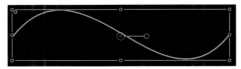

The Paint Stroke tool's default appearance is not
impressive, but the possibilities are incredible.

Modifying a Paint Stroke

The magic of the Paint Stroke tool is in its available parameters. Motion includes many preset brush styles to get you started. And like other elements in Motion, you can customize presets to make them your own.

The Shape Style pop-up menu (in the HUD and in the Inspector) provides access to many preset brushes.

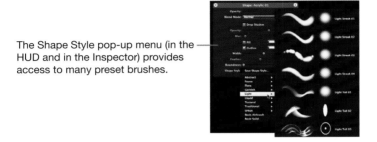

With a paint stroke selected, the Stroke and Advanced panes of the Shape tab become active.

Choose one of three settings for the Stroke Color Mode:

Allows for only an opacity change across the stroke.

Randomly applies a color to the stroke from the gradient editor.

Colorizes across the length of the stroke according to the pattern in the gradient editor.

See the earlier section on "Modifying a Closed Shape" for more information about the gradient editor.

Add random spacing to the dabs of a paint stroke. Animating this parameter creates a particle system look.

Access a curve-based editor to modify these parameters. See the *Motion User Manual* for more details.

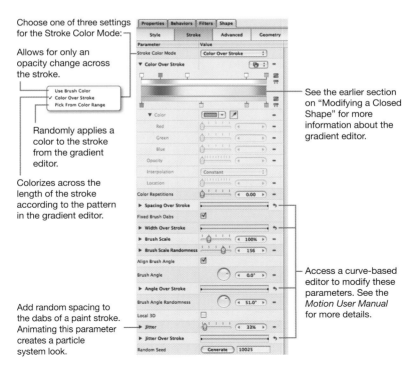

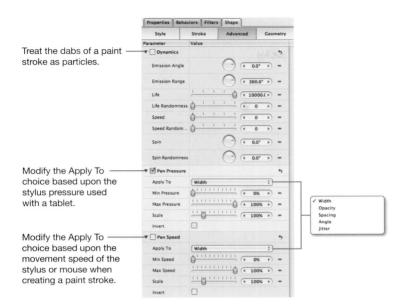

Treat the dabs of a paint stroke as particles.

Modify the Apply To choice based upon the stylus pressure used with a tablet.

Modify the Apply To choice based upon the movement speed of the stylus or mouse when creating a paint stroke.

Modifying the Control Points of a Shape, Mask, or Paint Stroke

After creating a common or custom shape, mask, or paint stroke, you can modify its control points to modify the object.

1   In the Layers tab or the Canvas, select the object you want to modify.

2   From the Toolbar, choose the Adjust Control Points tool.

3   Adjust, add, or delete points in the Canvas.

Move a point by dragging it in the Canvas. The pointer will become a crosshair.

Add a point by moving the pointer over the shape's outline at the location of the desired point, and then click when the pen icon has a plus sign.

Delete a point by Control-clicking (right-clicking) the point and choosing Delete Point.

Using Shape Behaviors

A few behaviors are specific to shapes. (See Chapter 7 for more information on applying behaviors.)

The first three behaviors work with information gleaned when creating a paint stroke with a graphics tablet. That information is then used with the associated parameters found in the Advanced pane of the Shape tab to modify the paint stroke. One application of this could be making a stroke wider when more pen pressure is used.

Oscillate Shape animates the control points by varying the points' positions within a range. This can result in very fluid motion.

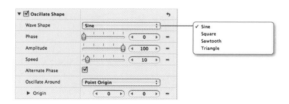

Randomize Shape creates a frenetic shape as the control points' positions randomly jump (offset) from their original locations.

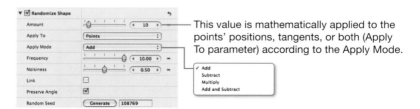

This value is mathematically applied to the points' positions, tangents, or both (Apply To parameter) according to the Apply Mode.

Sequence Paint is the only behavior that animates the individual dabs of a stroke. The functionality is very similar to the Sequence Text and Sequence Replicator behaviors.

1   Apply the Sequence Paint behavior to the paint stroke.

2   From the Parameter Add pop-up menu, choose the parameter you want to animate.

3   Modify the parameter's value as desired.

4   Change the controls as desired.

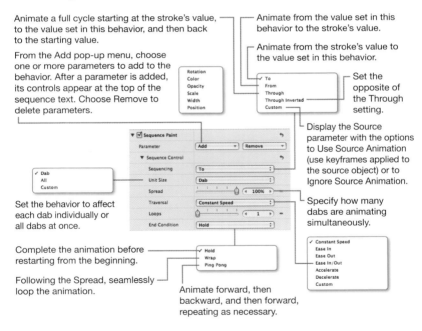

Animate a full cycle starting at the stroke's value, to the value set in this behavior, and then back to the starting value.

From the Add pop-up menu, choose one or more parameters to add to the behavior. After a parameter is added, its controls appear at the top of the sequence text. Choose Remove to delete parameters.

Animate from the value set in this behavior to the stroke's value.

Animate from the stroke's value to the value set in this behavior.

Set the opposite of the Through setting.

Display the Source parameter with the options to Use Source Animation (use keyframes applied to the source object) or to Ignore Source Animation.

Set the behavior to affect each dab individually or all dabs at once.

Specify how many dabs are animating simultaneously.

Complete the animation before restarting from the beginning.

Following the Spread, seamlessly loop the animation.

Animate forward, then backward, and then forward, repeating as necessary.

Track Points allows you to lock the control points of a shape or mask to the movement within video content or to another animated object. See the *Motion User Manual* for more information.

Wriggle Shape animates the control points in a way similar to randomize, but without the caffeine. Control-click (or right-click) a control point to disable it from modification by this behavior.

Write On is a quick way to reveal a paint stroke or outline over time and stroke rather than applying the basic Fade In/Fade Out behavior.

4
Particles and Replicators

The particle and replicator engines in Motion make it easy to add dynamic and complex animations to projects. Particles are great for creating environmental effects such as rain, smoke, or fire; replicators can be used to create textures, animated patterns, or even video walls. While Motion ships with hundreds of particle and replicator presets, almost any visual object can be turned into a particle/replicator system.

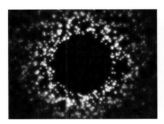 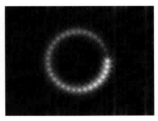

The same source object was used to create the particles on the left and the replicator on the right.

Particle System

A particle system comprises two parts: an emitter that "spits out" the particle cells, and a life cycle that determines when particles are born, live, and die. The visible part of the cycle and the particle's behavior during each phase of that cycle is highly customizable in Motion.

Using Preset Particle Systems

1   In the Utility window, click the Library tab.

2   In the Library tab, choose Particle Emitters and, if desired, a specific subcategory.

3 Select the desired preset from the file stack.

> **TIP** Click a preset to preview the particle system. Press the Up or Down Arrow keys to select and preview other particle systems.

4 To add the preset to your project, select a destination group, if desired, and then do one of the following:

▸ Click the Apply button at the top of the Library tab.

▸ Drag the preset to the desired group within the Layers tab.

▸ Drag the preset to the Canvas or Timeline.

Preview the Particle Emitter preset selected in the file stack.

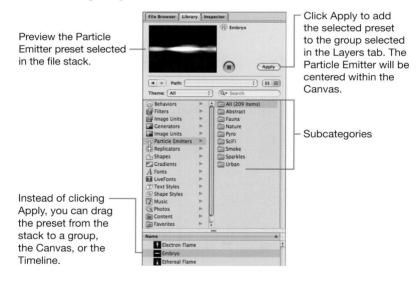

Click Apply to add the selected preset to the group selected in the Layers tab. The Particle Emitter will be centered within the Canvas.

Subcategories

Instead of clicking Apply, you can drag the preset from the stack to a group, the Canvas, or the Timeline.

> **TIP** By default, the preset is timed to start at the playhead if playback is stopped; otherwise, the preset starts at the beginning of the project.

Creating a Particle System

1 In the Canvas window or Layers tab, select a source object to become the particle cell.

Source object

TIP ▶ Any visual element (still, shape, text, video, or group) can be turned into a particle cell.

2   In the Toolbar, click the Make Particles icon, or press E.

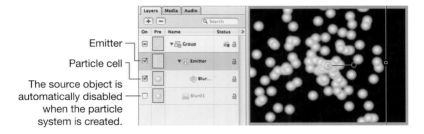

Emitter

Particle cell

The source object is automatically disabled when the particle system is created.

Modifying a Particle System

The Inspector tab allows you to customize the appearance and behavior of a particle system. As when modifying other layers in Motion, note which layer is selected—a particle cell or the emitter—before making adjustments.

NOTE ▶ If more than one particle cell is applied and selected, the particle cell parameter list for the emitter will be truncated to a master controls list.

TIP ▶ The HUD displays a reduced selection of parameters for adjusting a particle system.

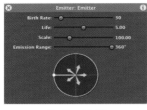

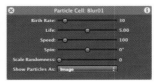

Emitter HUD   Particle Cell HUD

Parameters of a Particle Cell

When a particle cell is selected in the Layers tab, the object tab will display as shown in the following figure. If the emitter is selected, these same parameters will appear in the lower portion of the Emitter tab in the Inspector.

Control how many particles are created per second.

Create a burst of particles at the beginning of the emitter.

Vary the length of each particle's life cycle.

Vary the velocity of each particle.

Vary the emission angle of each particle.

Vary the spin amount for each particle.

Color Mode has five options. Refer to the following images for more information.

Click the disclosure triangle to set X and Y independently.

A 0% value gives particles a path independent of the emitter's movement. A 100% value creates a "cloud" of particles that surround the emitter as it moves.

Two emitters with the same settings will animate the same way when their Random Seed values are identical. Click Generate to create a new random pattern with a similar look.

View the source object for this particle cell. Drag a different source object to this image well to change the source object.

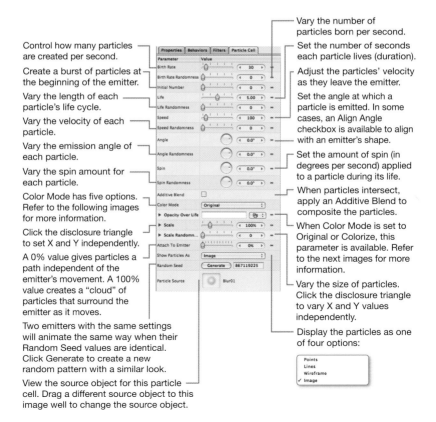

Vary the number of particles born per second.

Set the number of seconds each particle lives (duration).

Adjust the particles' velocity as they leave the emitter.

Set the angle at which a particle is emitted. In some cases, an Align Angle checkbox is available to align with an emitter's shape.

Set the amount of spin (in degrees per second) applied to a particle during its life.

When particles intersect, apply an Additive Blend to composite the particles.

When Color Mode is set to Original or Colorize, this parameter is available. Refer to the next images for more information.

Vary the size of particles. Click the disclosure triangle to vary X and Y values independently.

Display the particles as one of four options:

Setting Color Mode to Original allows adjustment of the particles' opacity over their life cycles.

Select a tag to adjust its settings. Drag the tag left or right to set its position in the particles' life cycles. Drag a tag off the bar to delete it.

Optionally, select or save a gradient preset.

Reverse a tag's position in the life cycle.

Click the bar to create additional tags.

Controls the interpolation of the tag: Constant, Linear, or Continuous.

Set the selected tag's position in the particles' life cycles using the Location slider, or by dragging the tag.

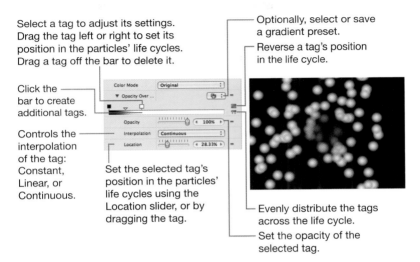

Evenly distribute the tags across the life cycle.

Set the opacity of the selected tag.

Setting Color Mode to Colorize allows tinting and alpha channel manipulation.

To choose a color for the particles, use the color well, the pop-up arrow, or the eyedropper; or drag the sliders.

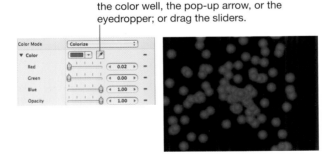

Setting Color Mode to Over Life affects the particles' life cycles from left to right in the gradient editor. The particles take the range of opacity and color tags from left to right as they are born, live, and then die.

Select a color tag before making adjustments below.

Repeat or loop the gradient pattern over the life of the particles.

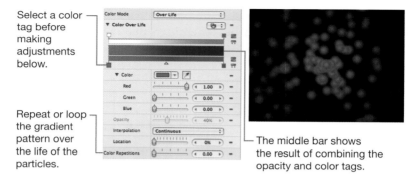

The middle bar shows the result of combining the opacity and color tags.

The particles will randomly select a color from the gradient editor.

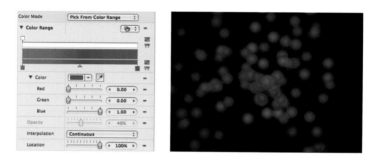

NOTE ▶ Additional parameters become available with other object types such as a movie object.

When Play Frames is selected, the particles play the movie.

Start each particle at a random frame of the movie.

Randomly add to or subtract from the Hold Frames value.

Repeat each frame of the movie during playback to create a slow-motion effect. A value of 5 plays a frame five times before moving to the next frame.

Emitter Shapes

Motion includes 11 preset shapes for emitters that can be customized for your project. Here are examples of the emitter shapes available:

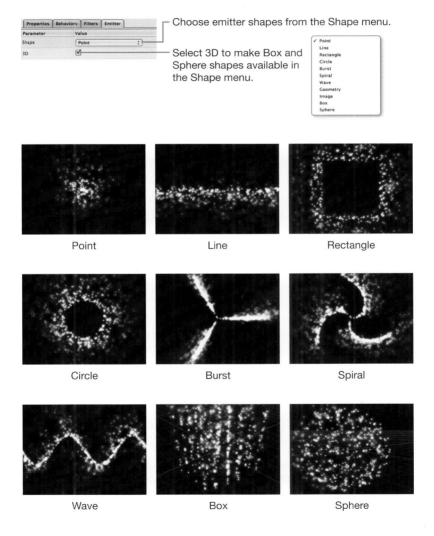

Choose emitter shapes from the Shape menu.

Select 3D to make Box and Sphere shapes available in the Shape menu.

Point	Line	Rectangle
Circle	Burst	Spiral
Wave	Box	Sphere

To use Geometry, create or choose a shape. Then, drag the shape from the Layers tab to the Shape Source image well. Disable the shape in the Layers tab, if desired.

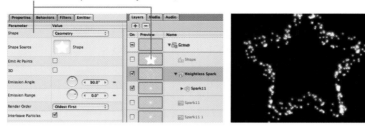

Behaviors and Filters for Particle Systems

As with any non-text layer, you can easily apply behaviors and filters to create movement or a particular appearance for a particle system. Behaviors and filters can be applied to the source object, the particle cell(s), or the emitter, each with a different result. Two behaviors are specific to particle systems: Scale Over Life and Spin Over Life.

NOTE ▶ Filters and behaviors cannot be applied to individual particle cells.

Four increment types are available: Natural Scale, Rate, "Birth and Death Values," and Custom.

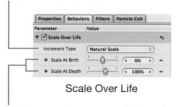

Scale Over Life

Scale parameters are available when Natural Scale or "Birth and Death Values" are chosen for Increment Type. When "Birth and Death Values" is chosen, these parameters are multiplied against the particle's pre-existing scale.

Three increment types are available: Rate, "Birth and Death Values," and Custom.

Spin Over Life

The Spin Rate sets a constant rate of rotation for particles. When "Birth and Death Values" is chosen, two parameters are displayed to adjust the spin amount at the birth and at the death of the particles.

Replicators

Like particle emitters, replicators create patterns from a chosen source object (image, shape, movie, text, generator, and so on), but replicators do not have an inherent life cycle. They are more struc-tured than particle systems, taking on a specific pattern or shape, yet used to create abstract backgrounds.

Using Preset Replicators

1   In the Utility window, select the Library tab.

2   In the Library tab, choose Replicators and, if desired, a specific subcategory.

3   Select the desired preset from the file stack.

> **TIP** Single-click a preset to preview the replicator at the top of the Library tab. Use the Up or Down Arrow keys to preview additional presets.

4   To add the preset to your project, select a destination group, if desired, and then do one of the following:

   ▶   Click the Apply button at the top of the Library tab.

   ▶   Drag the preset to the desired group within the Layers tab.

   ▶   Drag the preset to the Canvas.

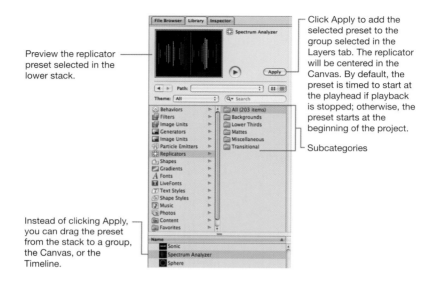

Preview the replicator preset selected in the lower stack.

Click Apply to add the selected preset to the group selected in the Layers tab. The replicator will be centered in the Canvas. By default, the preset is timed to start at the playhead if playback is stopped; otherwise, the preset starts at the beginning of the project.

Subcategories

Instead of clicking Apply, you can drag the preset from the stack to a group, the Canvas, or the Timeline.

Creating a Replicator from Scratch

1   In the Canvas window or Layers tab, select a source object to become the replicator cell.

Source object

TIP Any visual element (still, graphic, text, video, or group) can be turned into a replicator cell.

2   In the Toolbar, click the Replicate icon, or press L.

Replicator —

Replicator cell —

Source object —
is automatically
disabled when
the replicator is
created.

TIP Cells can be added to a replicator by dragging an additional source object to the replicator in the Layers tab.

Modifying a Replicator

The Inspector tab allows you to customize the appearance of a replicator. As when modifying other layers in Motion, note which layer is selected before making adjustments.

TIP The HUD displays a reduced selection of parameters for adjusting the replicator.

Replicator HUD   Replicator cell HUD

Parameters of a Replicator Cell

Set the angle of the cells on the pattern. In some cases, an Align Angle checkbox is available to align with the replicator's shape.

Vary the rotation for each cell.

Five Color Mode settings are available. See the following images for more information.

Click the disclosure triangle to set X and Y values independently.

Vary the size of particles. Click the disclosure triangle to vary X and Y values independently.

Two replicators with the same Random Seed settings will animate in the same way when this value, and other parameters, are the same. Click Generate to create a new random pattern with a similar appearance.

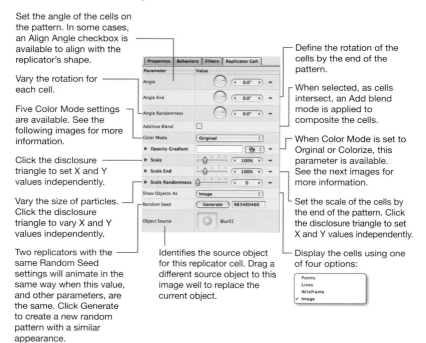

Define the rotation of the cells by the end of the pattern.

When selected, as cells intersect, an Add blend mode is applied to composite the cells.

When Color Mode is set to Orginal or Colorize, this parameter is available. See the next images for more information.

Set the scale of the cells by the end of the pattern. Click the disclosure triangle to set X and Y values independently.

Identifies the source object for this replicator cell. Drag a different source object to this image well to replace the current object.

Display the cells using one of four options:

NOTE ▶ All Color Modes are affected by the Origin parameter set in the Replicator tab. Origin sets the anchor point of the pattern at Center by default.

When Color Mode is set to Original, you can adjust the cells' opacity over the pattern.

Select a tag to adjust its settings. Drag the tag left or right to set its position in the particles' life cycles. Drag a tag off the bar to delete it.

Optionally, select or save a gradient preset.

Reverse a tag's position in the life cycle.

Click the bar to create additional tags.

Controls the interpolation of the tag: Constant, Linear, or Continuous.

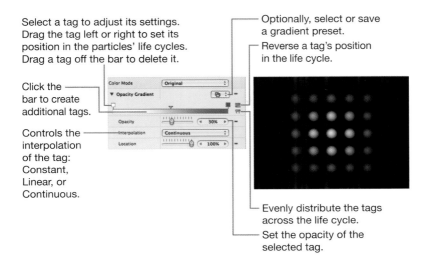

Evenly distribute the tags across the life cycle.

Set the opacity of the selected tag.

When Color Mode is set to Colorize, you can adjust tinting and manipulate the alpha channel.

Use one of these three controls (the color well, the pop-up arrow, or the eyedropper) or use the sliders below to pick the color to apply to the replicator.

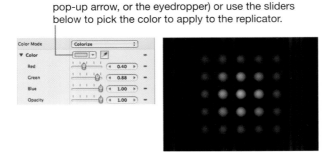

When Color Mode is set to Over Pattern, the cells are modified by the Origin parameter in the Replicator tab. The cells take the range of opacity and color tags from left to right across the pattern.

Select a color tag before making adjustments.

Repeat or loop the gradient over the pattern.

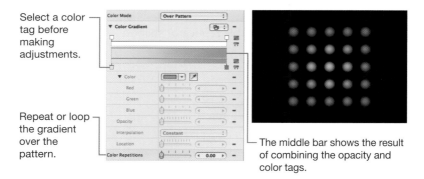

The middle bar shows the result of combining the opacity and color tags.

When Color Mode is set to Pick From Color Range, the cells randomly select a color from the gradient editor regardless of the Origin setting.

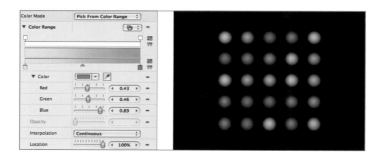

NOTE ▸ Additional parameters become available with other object types, such as a movie object.

When Play Frames is selected, the cells play the movie. When deselected, the cells are still frames. The parameters in this figure are available when the source object is a movie.

Select the starting frame of the source movie.

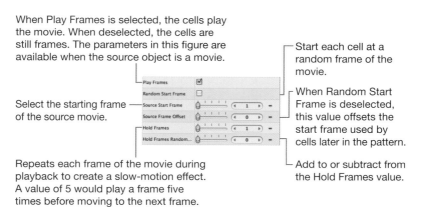

Start each cell at a random frame of the movie.

When Random Start Frame is deselected, this value offsets the start frame used by cells later in the pattern.

Repeats each frame of the movie during playback to create a slow-motion effect. A value of 5 would play a frame five times before moving to the next frame.

Add to or subtract from the Hold Frames value.

Replicator Shapes

Here are examples of the available replicator shapes:

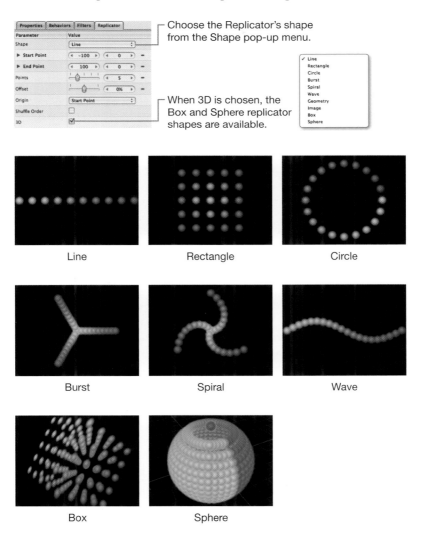

Choose the Replicator's shape from the Shape pop-up menu.

When 3D is chosen, the Box and Sphere replicator shapes are available.

Line   Rectangle   Circle

Burst   Spiral   Wave

Box   Sphere

To use Geometry, create or choose a shape. Then, drag the shape from the Layers tab to the Shape Source image well. Disable the shape in the Layers tab, if desired.

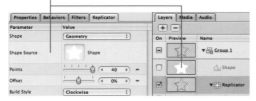 

Behaviors and Filters for Replicators

As with any non-text layer, you may easily apply behaviors and filters to create movement or a particular appearance for replicators. The Basic Motion, Parameter, and Simulation behaviors can be applied to a replicator. Within the Basic Motion subcategory, only Throw and Spin may be applied to replicator cells.

One behavior applies only to replicators or replicator cells: Sequence Replicator. This powerful behavior requires customization.

1 Apply the Sequence Replicator behavior to a replicator.

2 From the Parameter Add pop-up menu, choose the parameter you want to animate.

3 Modify the parameter's values to the desired settings.

4 Change the Sequence controls as desired.

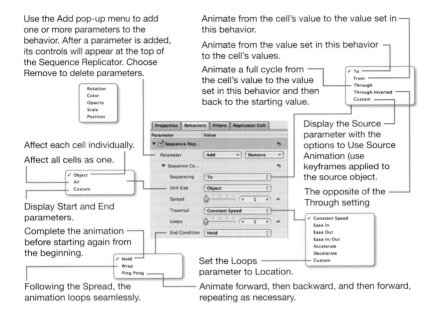

Use the Add pop-up menu to add one or more parameters to the behavior. After a parameter is added, its controls will appear at the top of the Sequence Replicator. Choose Remove to delete parameters.

Animate from the cell's value to the value set in this behavior.

Animate from the value set in this behavior to the cell's values.

Animate a full cycle from the cell's value to the value set in this behavior and then back to the starting value.

Display the Source parameter with the options to Use Source Animation (use keyframes applied to the source object.

The opposite of the Through setting

Affect each cell individually.

Affect all cells as one.

Display Start and End parameters.

Complete the animation before starting again from the beginning.

Set the Loops parameter to Location.

Following the Spread, the animation loops seamlessly.

Animate forward, then backward, and then forward, repeating as necessary.

For example, if you wanted to fade-in the particle cells across the pattern, do the following:

1   Choose Add > Opacity.

2   Change the Opacity value to 0.

3   Set Sequencing to From.

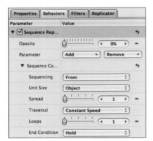

4   Adjust the behavior's duration in the mini-Timeline.

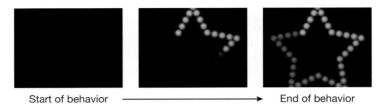

Start of behavior ⟶ End of behavior

TIP▸ You can animate more than one parameter by choosing additional parameters from the Add pop-up menu.

5

Timelines

Motion has two timelines: the mini-Timeline at the bottom of the Canvas and the Timeline tab in the Timing pane. The mini-Timeline displays only the duration and time position of a selected object. The Timeline allows you to manipulate many components of your project at once. While applications such as After Effects use their timelines extensively, the Motion Timeline is used primarily to make global changes and perform simple project edits.

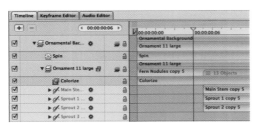

The Timeline reflects the vertical stacking of the Layers tab with the timebars describing the horizontal components for each layer in project time.

Working in the Mini-Timeline

The mini-Timeline is always visible at the bottom of the Canvas. Here you can add and adjust the timing/duration of a selected object, filter, or behavior.

> **TIP** Several of the mini-Timeline functions are also available in the Timeline.

Adding Single Objects

Single objects can be dragged directly from the utility window to the mini-Timeline. When you drag a new object to the mini-Timeline, a tooltip appears to indicate where the object will be placed in the project.

Adding Multiple Objects

You can select multiple objects and add them to the mini-Timeline. You have two options when adding multiple objects: Composite and Sequential.

1   From the File Browser tab or Library tab, select multiple objects.

2   Drag the selected objects to the mini-Timeline, but don't release the mouse button. After a pause, the drop menu appears.

3   Position the pointer over the desired import option and release the mouse button.

Choosing a Composite import stacks the objects into separate layers with their In points at the drop point. The mini-Timeline displays the shaded area to indicate that multiple objects are selected.

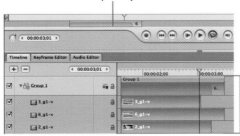

In this example, the Timeline is visible to compare against the mini-Timeline's representation of the import.

Choosing a Sequential import puts each object into separate layers, but In points are delayed by the duration of the preceding object.

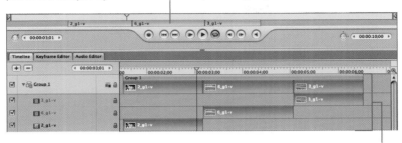

In this example, the Timeline is visible to compare against the mini-Timeline's representation of the import.

NOTE ▶ The order in which your objects are placed into your project is based on the order that you selected them in the File Browser or Library.

Moving Objects

Moving clips in the mini-Timeline is as simple as dragging them to a new location. When dragging clips, a tooltip appears to indicate the In point, the Out point, and the delta value (length of the change).

NOTE ▶ Drag the middle of the clip—not the edges.

TIP ▶ When moving clips, press N to turn snapping on and off.

Trimming Objects

Trimming applies to groups and layers (anything selected in your project that has a timebar). You have two main ways to trim an object:

▶ Place the playhead at the desired location for the selected object and press I to trim the In point or O to trim the Out point to the playhead.

Before ⟶ After pressing the O key

▶ Place the pointer at the beginning or end of the selected object. When the pointer changes to the trim pointer, drag to trim the object.

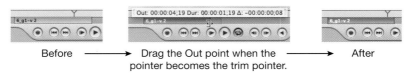

Before ⟶ Drag the Out point when the ⟶ After
pointer becomes the trim pointer.

TIP By pressing Command when trimming a group or layer, you will not change any effects that have been applied.

Retiming Clips

You can easily retime clips in the mini-Timeline.

1   Place the mouse pointer at the end of a clip and hold down the Option key.

2   Drag the clip's Out point left or right to the desired speed/duration value, and then release the mouse button.

The retime pointer appears with a tooltip that displays the speed and duration change.

Looping Clips

Looping is best used on video objects that have been designed to return seamlessly from the last frame to first frame. But, you can loop any clip in Motion.

1   Place the mouse pointer over a clip's Out point.

2   Option-Shift-drag the Out point to the right to create the loop, and then release the mouse button.

A loop point barrier indicates where the loop begins.

Working in the Timeline

The Timeline tab is located in the Timing pane. You can open the Timing pane by pressing F6, or go directly to the Timeline tab by pressing Command-7. You can resize the open Timing pane by dragging the divider bar between it and the mini-Timeline.

TIP Some of the following functions also work in the mini-Timeline.

Adding Objects

Depending on where you drag objects on the Timeline, you have up to four choices for adding objects. All choices will create a new Timeline track.

Also, the pointer location when you release the mouse button determines the placement of an object added to the Timeline (horizontally and vertically).

Did you release the pointer with the new clip as shown in the left image or as shown in the right image? These two vertical positions will present slightly different import options and affect the layer order.

NOTE ▶ If you drag multiple objects, you will be able to choose Composite or Sequential from the drop menu (as in the mini-Timeline).

You may have these four import options in the Timeline (depending on vertical placement) when adding an object:

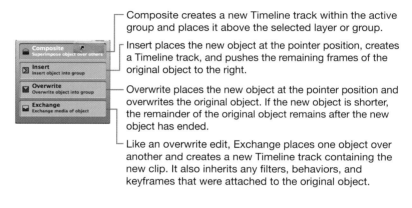

Composite creates a new Timeline track within the active group and places it above the selected layer or group.

Insert places the new object at the pointer position, creates a Timeline track, and pushes the remaining frames of the original object to the right.

Overwrite places the new object at the pointer position and overwrites the original object. If the new object is shorter, the remainder of the original object remains after the new object has ended.

Like an overwrite edit, Exchange places one object over another and creates a new Timeline track containing the new clip. It also inherits any filters, behaviors, and keyframes that were attached to the original object.

NOTE ▶ Exchange works only with similar media. For example, you can't exchange a QuickTime movie with a generator.

Moving an Object to the Playhead
You can easily move the In or Out point of a selection to your current playhead position.

NOTE ▶ This function moves an object's time position. It does not trim the object's duration. See "Trimming Objects" in this chapter.

1 Move the playhead to the desired location.

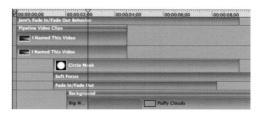

2   Press Shift-[(Left Bracket) to move the start of the selected objects to the playhead position.

TIP ▶ Optionally, press Shift-] (Right Bracket) to move the end of the selection to the playhead position and essentially backtime the objects.

Splitting Clips

Splitting a clip is like using the Blade tool in Final Cut Pro. It cuts a clip into two separate objects. In Motion, however, a new Timeline track is created when you split the clip.

1   Select one or more objects.

2   Place the playhead where you want to perform the split.

3   From the menu bar, choose Edit > Split.

A new Timeline track is created for the split clip and any associated filters/behaviors.

Slipping Clips

In the process of trimming, you may have removed material you want to play within the new clip duration. Motion has a Slip tool that reveals all of the source material and allows you to modify both the In and Out points simultaneously.

1 Place the pointer over the middle of a clip.

2 Option-drag to the left or right until the desired footage is visible within the clip's duration.

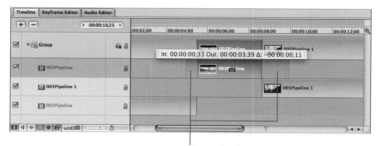

When slipping, you will see the handles
(the unused source material) of your object.

TIP When slipping objects, place the playhead at the beginning or end of your object so that you can see the new In or Out point in the Canvas.

Creating Time Regions

Time regions allow you to select a range of your project in the Timeline ruler or in an individual Timeline track. They function much like the Range Selection tool in Final Cut Pro. In Motion, however, you can select one or more tracks depending on where you create the region.

1 Command-Option-drag to create a time region.

2   After creating a time region, place the pointer over its left or
right side to modify the region.

TIP ▶ After creating a time region, you can Command-click
Timeline tracks to select and deselect additional tracks.

3   When you have selected an object in the Timeline or created a
time region, you can delete that content by pressing Delete.

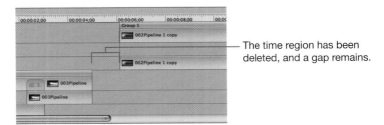

The time region has been
deleted, and a gap remains.

To avoid leaving a gap, you can press Shift-Delete to perform a
ripple delete. This will delete the selection and ripple the subse-
quent content to the left, thereby removing the gap.

Working with Markers

Markers allow you to add visual references and notes to your entire project or to specific objects. Project markers can also perform specific tasks when flagged properly.

Project and Object Markers

Project markers are visible in the Timeline ruler, and unlike object markers, they are also displayed in the mini-Timeline as green vertical lines.

Press Shift-M to create a project marker at the playhead position.

Select an object and press M to create an object marker at the playhead position.

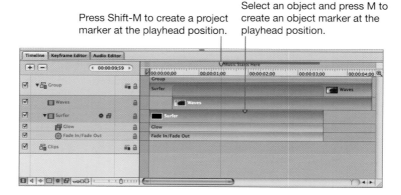

Editing Marker Information

The Edit Marker dialog allows you to add specific information to your markers and to flag them for special use.

1   Double-click a marker to open the Edit Marker dialog.

2   In the dialog, edit information about your marker and choose a visual duration that is displayed in the Timeline.

In the Type pop-up menu, you can flag a marker to be used in DVD Studio Pro as a DVD menu loop point or an alpha transition.

6
Keyframes

While behaviors and parameter behaviors permit a tremendous amount of control over animation in Motion, at times an object's parameters can be more precisely animated using keyframes. Whether changing an object's color or animating a filter or light, keyframes can create very specific animations quickly and easily, with additional control provided by the Motion Keyframe Editor.

Just about everything in Motion can be keyframed.
That's a lot of animation possibilities.

Setting Keyframes Manually

When a project requires only a few keyframes, it may be easiest to create them manually from the Animation menu. This process also uses the playhead and the Inspector.

1   Place the playhead where a keyframe is needed.

2   In the Inspector, click the Animation menu next to the parameter that needs to be keyframed.

3   From the pop-up menu, choose Add Keyframe.

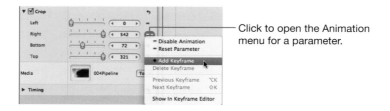

Click to open the Animation menu for a parameter.

4   Repeat steps 2 and 3 for any additional parameters that require a keyframe at the playhead's position, and then proceed to step 5.

5   Move the playhead to the next position where you want to apply keyframes.

6   From the Animation menu, choose Add Keyframe for any parameters that require a keyframe at the playhead's current position.

7   After setting the keyframes, adjust the parameter settings as desired.

8   Repeat steps 5 through 7 as necessary to further define your animation.

NOTE ▸ Set a keyframe before adjusting the parameter's setting.

The Animation menu's icon indicates the keyframed status of a parameter.

▬ —— No keyframes exist for this parameter.

◆ —— A keyframe exists before or after the playhead's location.

◆ —— A keyframe has been created at the playhead's location.

TIP ▸ Option-click the Animation menu to create a keyframe at the playhead position without opening the pop-up menu.

Using Record Animation to Create Keyframes

The Record Animation feature allows for keyframes to be recorded automatically when making changes to a project—in other words, a hybrid version of manual and automatic keyframing. Although this can make animating extremely fast, knowing how to use the feature will prevent a lot of unwanted keyframes in your projects.

1   Double-click the Record button.

2   In the Recording Options window that appears, set the desired options.

Keyframe Thinning options determine how many keyframes are recorded in real time.

Deselect to record keyframes in real time as the project plays back.

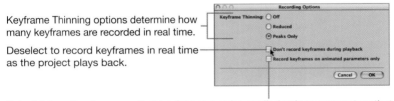

Select this option to ensure that keyframes can be applied only to parameters that already have keyframes. This option is specific to Record Animation. By manually adding keyframes, you can still apply keyframes to any parameter.

3   Ensure that recording is activated. The Record button will pulsate red.

4   Now you have two options: advance the playhead manually or start playback.

▶   If you want to advance manually, cue the playhead and then adjust an object's parameters in the Canvas, Inspector, HUD, Timeline, or Keyframe Editor. Cue the playhead to the next frame that needs keyframes, and then adjust the parameters. Keyframes are recorded for each change.

▶   Alternatively, you could start playback and then adjust an object's parameters in the Canvas, Inspector, Timeline, or Keyframe Editor during playback. Keyframes are recorded for each change.

The result of recording keyframes during playback. The light was animated to follow the surfer. The keyframes now can be modified in the Canvas, Inspector, Timeline, or Keyframe Editor.

5   Click the Record button to stop recording.

Using the Keyframe Editor

The Keyframe Editor acts as command central when applying and working with keyframes in Motion. It allows precise control over animation curves.

Creating Keyframes

To keyframe a parameter:

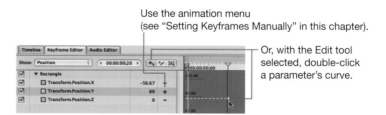

Use the animation menu
(see "Setting Keyframes Manually" in this chapter).

Or, with the Edit tool selected, double-click a parameter's curve.

NOTE ▶ You can also use the Sketch tool to draw a keyframe curve for a parameter.

Editing Keyframes

In addition to editing single keyframes with the Edit tool, you can edit multiple keyframes using the Box tool.

1 Choose the Box tool.

2 Drag within the Keyframe Editor to select the keyframes you want to modify.

3 Drag the selected keyframes left or right to adjust their timings. Drag keyframes up or down to change their parameters' values.

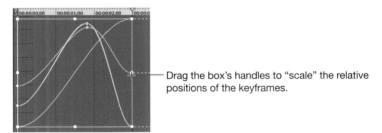

Drag the box's handles to "scale" the relative positions of the keyframes.

> **TIP** ▶ To modify a single keyframe, you can drag the keyframe vertically or double-click the keyframe and type a parameter value.

Setting a Keyframe's Interpolation

Interpolation determines the transition that occurs between and through keyframes, and it creates the "feel" of animated parameters. For example, if the interpolation for a keyframe is set to Ease Out, the animation will begin more slowly as it comes out of a keyframe, whereas an Ease In interpolation will make an animation end more slowly going into a keyframe.

To change interpolation, Control-click (or right-click) a keyframe and choose an interpolation from the shortcut menu. Here are some examples of interpolation options:

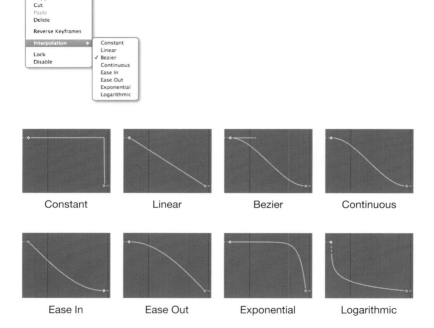

Constant	Linear	Bezier	Continuous

Ease In	Ease Out	Exponential	Logarithmic

Taking Curve Snapshots

Curve snapshots maintain a record of original animation curves when you change keyframe positions in the curve graph. By taking a curve snapshot, you not only preserve a reference to the original curve, but you also enable the ability to restore that curve.

1   At the lower left of the Keyframe Editor, click the "Take/Show Curve Snapshot" button.

Take/Show Curve Snapshot button

2   Adjust the curves to the new values.

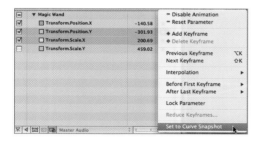

As you adjust the keyframes, the old curves appear in a lighter shade.

3   If you want to revert to the previous values, select the parameters of the modified curves, and from the Animation menu, choose Set to Curve Snapshot.

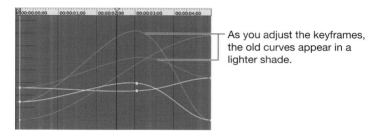

NOTE ▶ Exiting the Keyframe Editor or changing to another set of curves will dispose of the previous snapshot.

Applying Extrapolation

Extrapolation determines the animation that occurs before the first keyframe and after the last keyframe of a parameter—as opposed to interpolation, which determines behavior between the keyframes.

Extrapolation can be especially useful to loop (repeat), extend, or ping-pong the animation in a project.

1   Create the first loop for a parameter.

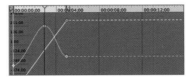

2   From the parameter's Animation menu, choose the desired extrapolation.

Motion creates the additional keyframes.

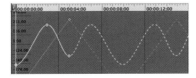

Using a Mini-Curve Editor

Motion's mini-curve editors are scaled-down versions of the Keyframe Editor. The mini-curve editors let you modify animation curves for certain parameters and appear for a few parameters when working with paint strokes and particle systems.

You can add, delete, and modify keyframes in a mini-curve editor.

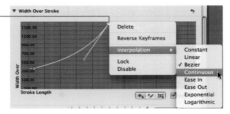

Modifying Keyframes in the Timeline

After creating keyframes, you may need to adjust their timings or even their parameters. In the Timeline, you can easily compare keyframes of multiple layers to adjust their relative timings.

1   Click the Show/Hide Keyframes button.

Show/Hide Keyframes

2   Adjust the keyframe as desired.

 Drag the keyframe left or right to align with other objects, keyframes, or markers as desired.

3   While you are editing in the Timeline:

▶   Hold down Shift to enable snapping.

▶   Control-click (or right-click) a keyframe, and from the shortcut menu, choose the value you want to change. Then enter a new value and press Return.

▶   You may also Control-click a keyframe and choose Delete Keyframes from the shortcut menu to remove the keyframe.

Converting Behaviors to Keyframes

Sometimes you apply behaviors to an object that don't offer the level of control you need over certain parameters. By converting those behaviors to keyframes, you can modify and edit the interpolation between keyframes and their curves.

1   Select the object (or group or layer) to which behaviors have been applied.

2   Choose Object > Convert to Keyframes.

3   From the Convert to Keyframes dialog, choose Convert.

⌐ Click Convert to change the behaviors
  to keyframe-based animations.

Because this conversion may yield many more keyframes than you want to deal with, you may need to reduce the number of keyframes.

4   In the Keyframe Editor, click the Animation menu for the parameter with extra keyframes.

5   From the Animation menu, choose Reduce Keyframes and enter values for keyframe reduction.

⌐ In this window you can choose the level
  of keyframe reduction. When you increase
  the Maximum Error Tolerance value, fewer
  keyframes are created. When you increase
  the Smoothing Factor value, smoother
  curves are created between the keyframes.

7

Behaviors

Behaviors are primarily used to animate objects. When you want to fade in an object, move a camera along a path, or animate text, behaviors allow you to do these things (and many others) without setting keyframes.

In a nutshell, there are two behavior types: "regular" and parameter. Regular behaviors (usually referred to simply as behaviors) can affect one or many parameters of an object. Parameter behaviors are applied to a single object parameter and, therefore, affect only that parameter.

Within the Motion interface, behaviors are grouped into 12 categories.

The icon view has only three behavior icons.

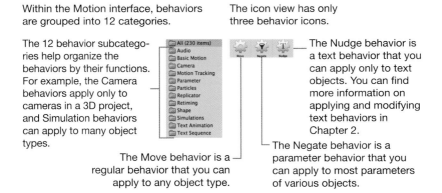

The 12 behavior subcategories help organize the behaviors by their functions. For example, the Camera behaviors apply only to cameras in a 3D project, and Simulation behaviors can apply to many object types.

The Move behavior is a regular behavior that you can apply to any object type.

The Nudge behavior is a text behavior that you can apply only to text objects. You can find more information on applying and modifying text behaviors in Chapter 2.

The Negate behavior is a parameter behavior that you can apply to most parameters of various objects.

Applying Behaviors

You have several methods for applying behaviors. This first method allows you to preview the various behaviors.

1   In the Layers tab or Canvas, select the destination object.

2   In the Inspector tab, select a behavior.

3 Apply the behavior using one of these options:

▶ Click the Apply button at the top of the Inspector.

▶ Drag the behavior to the destination object in the Layers tab or Canvas.

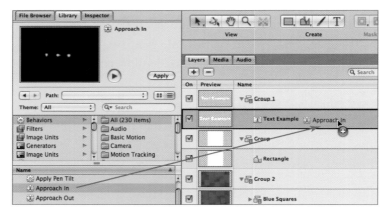

TIP A behavior takes on the duration of the destination object.

When you know which behavior you need, the following method provides quick access using the toolbar.

1 Select the destination object.

2 From the Behaviors pop-up menu in the Toolbar, choose the desired behavior.

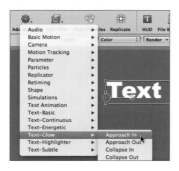

Modifying Behaviors

After you've applied a behavior, you may need to tweak its settings. You'll find the parameters of the selected behavior in the Behaviors tab of the Inspector and in the HUD.

NOTE ▶ The available parameters will vary for different behaviors.

All parameters for a behavior are displayed in the Inspector. As shown here, sometimes the HUD enables easier adjustment of those parameters.

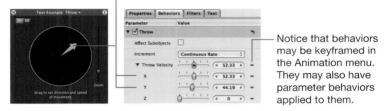

Notice that behaviors may be keyframed in the Animation menu. They may also have parameter behaviors applied to them.

You can move or duplicate a behavior from one object to another.

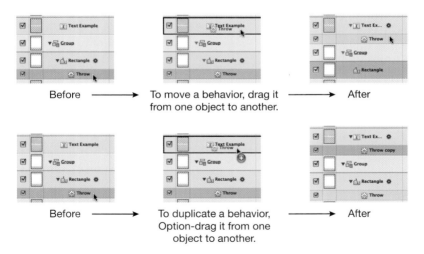

You can adjust a behavior's timing and duration in the mini-Timeline or Timeline, just as you would modify other objects.

To change a behavior's duration:

1 Place the Select/Transform tool on the behavior's In or Out point.

2 Drag the point to change the duration.

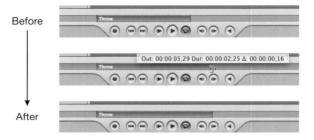

To alter the timing of a behavior relative to the applied object:

1 Place the Select/Transform tool in the middle of the behavior.

2 Drag to change the behavior's timing.

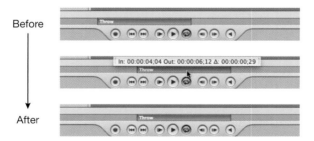

Example Behaviors

In this section, you'll examine examples of some specific behavior uses. (You will also find behaviors specific to text, shapes, paint strokes, particle systems, and replicators in their respective chapters of this book.)

Retiming

Several Retiming behaviors are available in Motion. They allow you to create flash frames, perform looped playback, and strobe and stutter clip playback. Set Speed is one Retiming behavior that allows you to create ramped speed effects within a clip.

This video clip is shown in the Timeline with the Set Speed behavior applied. The behavior's parameters are shown in the HUD.

During the duration of this behavior, the clip will play back at 50% speed (slow-motion).

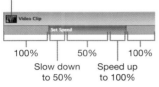

100%   50%   100%

Slow down   Speed up
to 50%   to 100%

The Ease In Time slider sets the number of frames over which the playback ramps from the clip's standard speed to the Speed value of the behavior. Ease In Curve determines the slope of the ramp: 0% is a linear slope.

Tracking

Tracking is a variant of the behaviors that, by themselves, do not "do" something to a video object. Instead, Tracking creates motion data about every pixel, such as determining where a pixel went from one frame to the next. This data may then be used to "attach" other objects such as graphics.

1   After applying the Tracking behavior, drag the default tracker to the video pixel you want to track.

2   If necessary, trim the behavior to the duration you need to track.

3 Before clicking Analyze, you can add another tracker by clicking Add.

Click the Analyze button to adjust the trackers' positions for each frame.

After analyzing the video, you will apply another behavior, Match Move, to a second object.

4 Apply Match Move to the "follow" object.

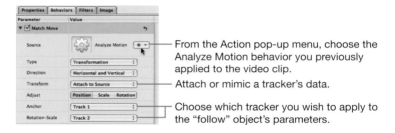

From the Action pop-up menu, choose the Analyze Motion behavior you previously applied to the video clip.

Attach or mimic a tracker's data.

Choose which tracker you wish to apply to the "follow" object's parameters.

NOTE ▶ Match Move can be used by itself as it has a built-in tracker. Match Move also has the ability to create a four-corner pin.

Stabilizing and Unstabilizing

As you can guess, these two behaviors do what their names imply. The Stabilize behavior can self-analyze a video clip or use tracker/tracker data to remove unwanted movement. The Unstabilize behavior can match new elements to original camera movement in a video clip. You must use tracker data created by another behavior (such as the Analyze Motion behavior) as the source of the camera movement.

Applying Parameter Behaviors

In addition to dragging parameter behaviors to apply them (as you would a regular behavior), you can also use the shortcut menus.

Control-click (or right-click) a parameter's name and then choose the parameter behavior from the shortcut menu.

Modifying Parameter Behaviors

Parameter behaviors appear in the Inspector's Behaviors tab. They are modified just like regular behaviors but have one special parameter: Apply To.

Use the Go pop-up menu to define the parameter affected by the parameter behavior.

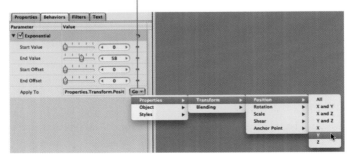

Example Parameter Behaviors

This section explores a few of the available parameter behaviors. See the *Motion 4 User Manual* for more information on all of the parameter behaviors.

Audio

The Audio parameter behavior allows you to animate an object's parameters according to the frequencies and amplitudes of an audio file.

1   Add an audio file to the project.

2   Select the object/group to be animated.

3   Control-click the parameter to be animated and choose Audio from the shortcut menu.

4   In the Behaviors tab of the Inspector, locate the Audio behavior you just added.

5   From the Source Audio To pop-up menu, choose the audio file to animate the parameter.

6   Adjust the parameters as desired.

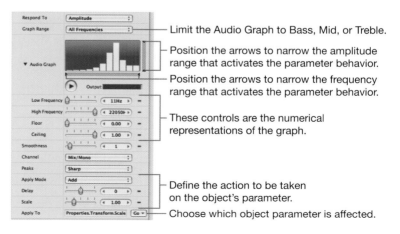

Limit the Audio Graph to Bass, Mid, or Treble.

Position the arrows to narrow the amplitude range that activates the parameter behavior.

Position the arrows to narrow the frequency range that activates the parameter behavior.

These controls are the numerical representations of the graph.

Define the action to be taken on the object's parameter.

Choose which object parameter is affected.

Link

When you need to animate one object in relation to another object's animation, the Link behavior can save you time and frustration. In essence, you are linking the behaviors applied to a parameter of one object to the same or even a different parameter of another object.

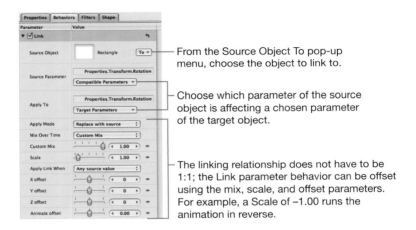

From the Source Object To pop-up menu, choose the object to link to.

Choose which parameter of the source object is affecting a chosen parameter of the target object.

The linking relationship does not have to be 1:1; the Link parameter behavior can be offset using the mix, scale, and offset parameters. For example, a Scale of –1.00 runs the animation in reverse.

Wriggle

It may have a funny name, but when you just need an object to jiggle, Wriggle is your go-to behavior.

1 Control-click a parameter to be animated and choose Wriggle from the shortcut menu.

2 In the Behaviors tab of the Inspector, adjust the parameters as desired.

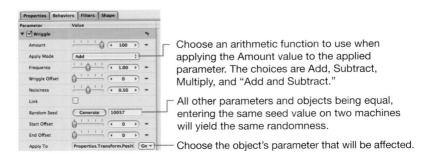

Choose an arithmetic function to use when applying the Amount value to the applied parameter. The choices are Add, Subtract, Multiply, and "Add and Subtract."

All other parameters and objects being equal, entering the same seed value on two machines will yield the same randomness.

Choose the object's parameter that will be affected.

The following figure illustrates the result of the Wriggle behavior applied to an object's Position parameter.

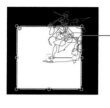

The shape's Position parameter is animated by adding up to 100 pixels to the X and Y parameters.

8

Filters

Filters allow you to create unique looks when applied to objects. They can be used to blur, sharpen, glow, key, matte, distort, and color correct objects, and much more. You can apply filters to one or more objects or entire groups. Filters are among the most often used creative tools in motion graphics.

Motion includes 13 categories of filters. With the ability to see results in real-time playback, choosing and adjusting a filter (such as the Levels filter shown here) becomes a fast and creative process.

NOTE ▸ Apply and modify filters judiciously. With 13 categories of filters that have a wide variety of parameters, it's easy to use too many filters or adjust them to extremes.

Applying Filters

You may apply filters to objects in many ways. When you want to preview filters, however, you should apply filters in the Library tab.

1   In the Layers tab or Canvas, select the destination object.

2   In the Library tab, select a filter.

3   Apply the filter using one of these two options:

▶   Click the Apply button at the top of the Inspector.

▶   Drag the filter to the destination object in the Layers tab or Canvas.

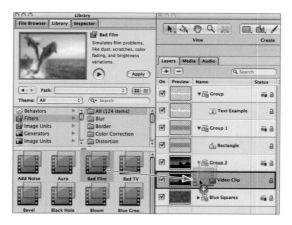

TIP ▶ A filter takes on the duration of the destination object.

When you already know which filter you need, you can use the Toolbar to get fast access to a specific filter.

1   Select the destination object.

2   In the Toolbar, click the Filters button, and then choose the desired filter.

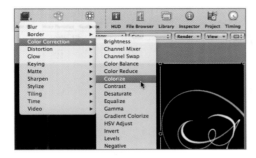

Modifying Filters

You can adjust a filter's parameters in the Filters subtab of the Inspector or in the HUD. The HUD usually contains a subset of a filter's available parameters. However, some filters, such as Levels, have no parameters displayed in the HUD.

NOTE ▶ The available parameters will vary from filter to filter.

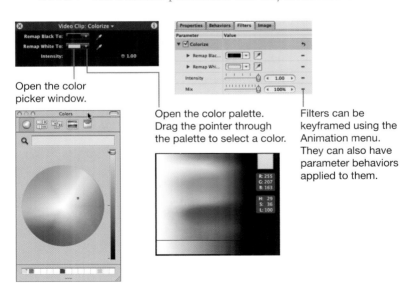

Open the color picker window.

Open the color palette. Drag the pointer through the palette to select a color.

Filters can be keyframed using the Animation menu. They can also have parameter behaviors applied to them.

While tweaking the look of an object, use the HUD to cycle between the object and applied behaviors and filters to make adjustments more quickly.

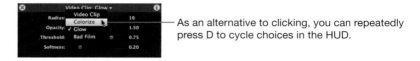

As an alternative to clicking, you can repeatedly press D to cycle choices in the HUD.

When applying multiple filters to an object, the order in which they are applied can yield different results. For instance, if you apply a Tint filter before a Light Rays filter, you'll get a different result than if you apply the Light Rays filter first. To change filter order, drag a filter to a new position in the Layers tab.

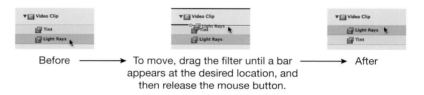

Before ⟶ To move, drag the filter until a bar ⟶ After
appears at the desired location, and
then release the mouse button.

After you've applied and adjusted one or more filters for an object, you may need to apply the same filter configuration to another object. Rather than redoing your work, you can copy filters and their settings.

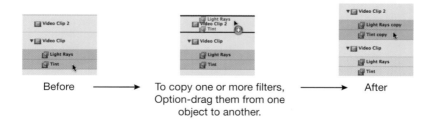

Before ⟶ To copy one or more filters, ⟶ After
Option-drag them from one
object to another.

The timing and duration of filters can be adjusted in the mini-Timeline or Timeline, just as you would adjust other objects.

To change a filter's duration:

1 Place the Select/Transform tool on the filter's In or Out point.

2 Drag to change the duration.

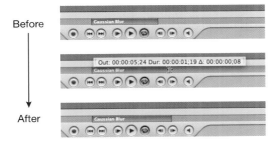

To alter the timing of a filter relative to the applied or other objects:

1 Place the Select/Transform tool in the middle of the filter.

2 Drag to change the filter timing.

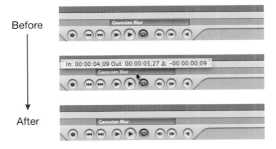

Filter Crop Parameter

When applying certain filters, you may notice that black is introduced around the edges of the Canvas area. This is because the filter is being applied at the source object's original boundaries.

If you notice dark edges around an object after applying a filter, go to the Filters Inspector and look for the Crop option. The filter's effect is limited to pixels within the object's frame size.

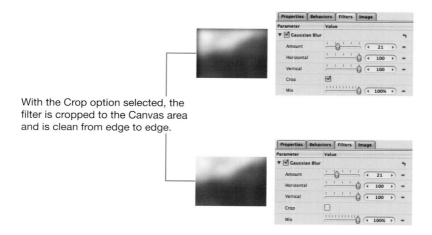

With the Crop option selected, the filter is cropped to the Canvas area and is clean from edge to edge.

Example Filters

Motion ships with filters that can be considered static or dynamic. Static filters may simply adjust the color of an object; dynamic filters modify pixels within the object over time. All filter types can be animated using keyframes and parameter behaviors. See Chapter 6, "Keyframes" and Chapter 7, "Behaviors," for more information on animating filters.

Here are a few of the filters included with Motion:

Gaussian Blur

The Gaussian Blur filter blurs the pixels of an object. Considered a static effect at its defaults, applying keyframes or parameter behaviors turns this filter into a dynamic effect.

The defaults blur pixels in both the horizontal and vertical directions. As shown here, you can choose to blur on only one axis.

Earthquake

The Earthquake filter is a dynamic effect found in the Distortion category. As the name implies, this filter makes the object appear as if shaken by an earthquake.

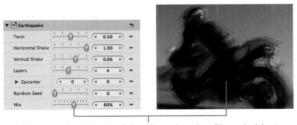

Mix controls a blend of the filtered and unfiltered object. A value of 100% outputs only the filtered object.

Bad Film

From the Stylize category, the Bad Film filter "grunges" your video to make it look like old or damaged film. As with any other dynamic effect, you will need to watch the filter's entire duration to ensure that the desired look is achieved. Setting a few or even one parameter too high could stylize your video beyond the desired effect.

As you can see here, some filters have more parameters than others. In some projects, taking a parameter to its maximum setting can become distracting, but don't be afraid to experiment with various settings.

9
Cameras and Views

Motion 2D projects have a default view—the active view—that shows what you see in the Canvas and what the exported file will contain. Adding a camera or cameras to your project creates many view options.

With a camera in your project, you can view objects from various angles.

Adding a Camera

You can add a camera to any project from the Toolbar.

1   In the Toolbar, click the New Camera icon.

2   If your project contains only 2D groups, a dialog appears.

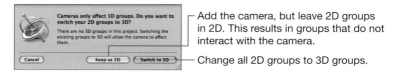

Add the camera, but leave 2D groups in 2D. This results in groups that do not interact with the camera.

Change all 2D groups to 3D groups.

TIP ▶ You can add multiple cameras to a project. With each camera placed at a different spatial location within the Canvas, you can cut between the camera angles during project playback.

When cameras overlap, the camera in the higher layer is the active camera.

Modifying a Camera

A camera has a few parameters to adjust in both the Inspector and the HUD. You can "change the lens" of the camera by modifying these settings.

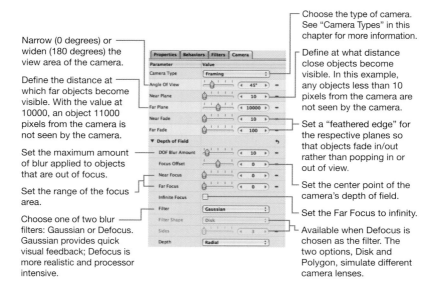

Choose the type of camera. See "Camera Types" in this chapter for more information.

Narrow (0 degrees) or widen (180 degrees) the view area of the camera.

Define the distance at which far objects become visible. With the value at 10000, an object 11000 pixels from the camera is not seen by the camera.

Set the maximum amount of blur applied to objects that are out of focus.

Set the range of the focus area.

Choose one of two blur filters: Gaussian or Defocus. Gaussian provides quick visual feedback; Defocus is more realistic and processor intensive.

Define at what distance close objects become visible. In this example, any objects less than 10 pixels from the camera are not seen by the camera.

Set a "feathered edge" for the respective planes so that objects fade in/out rather than popping in or out of view.

Set the center point of the camera's depth of field.

Set the Far Focus to infinity.

Available when Defocus is chosen as the filter. The two options, Disk and Polygon, simulate different camera lenses.

TIP Depth of Field parameters are enabled or disabled in the Render pop-up menu in the Canvas.

Camera Types

The two camera types, Framing and Viewpoint, are differentiated by their anchor points. The anchor point affects how the camera responds when you move the camera and is particularly important when rotating the camera.

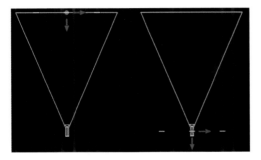

Framing camera, the default camera type, has an anchor point on the camera's focal plane.

A Viewpoint camera's anchor point is centered on the camera. This location makes the camera behave as if it is placed on a tripod.

Positioning a Camera

As with any other object in a 3D group, a camera may be moved using the Transform controls. Moving the camera with these controls requires using a view other than the camera view.

1   Select a camera in the Layers tab.

2   Choose the Adjust 3D Transform tool.

3   From the Camera menu, choose a different view, such as Perspective.

4   Drag the Canvas controls to adjust the camera's orientation.

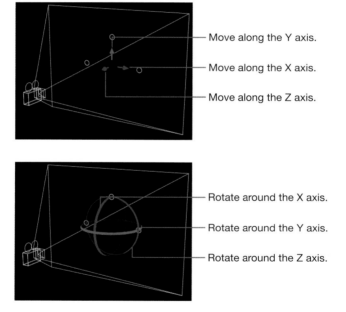

Move along the Y axis.

Move along the X axis.

Move along the Z axis.

Rotate around the X axis.

Rotate around the Y axis.

Rotate around the Z axis.

TIP ▸ To freely rotate, Command-drag a rotation handle (circle).

These camera adjustments also may be performed using the HUD controls.

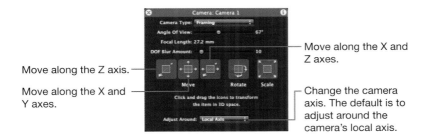

Move along the Z axis.

Move along the X and Y axes.

Move along the X and Z axes.

Change the camera axis. The default is to adjust around the camera's local axis.

Walk Camera Tool

An alternative to using the mouse to position a camera is the Walk Camera tool. Although you can drag in the Canvas with the tool, you can also perform camera adjustments using the keyboard.

1   In the Layers tab, select the camera.

2   From the Toolbar, choose the Walk Camera tool.

3   Press the Up, Down, Left, and Right Arrow keys to move the camera.

> **TIP** ▶ Hold down the Option key while pressing the arrow keys to move the camera in smaller increments.

3D View Tools

A third method of moving a camera also adjusts the selected view. To use these tools, you must drag the pointer on the tool itself.

The scene camera indicator appears when you are manipulating the active camera. Otherwise, the tools adjust the view in the Camera menu.

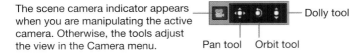

Dolly tool

Pan tool   Orbit tool

Camera Behaviors

In addition to using basic behaviors, such as Throw and Motion Path, cameras can receive behaviors specifically for animation. You can add behaviors to a camera as you would add a behavior to any object. (See Chapter 7, "Behaviors," for more information.)

Dolly
Move the camera along its Z axis to "push in" or "pull out."

Focus
Animate the Focus Offset parameter to create a rack-focus effect.

Framing
Create a customizable motion path that ends with the camera framing the target object.

Sweep
Animate the camera in an arc.

Zoom In/Out
Adjust the camera's Angle of View parameter.

Zoom Layer
Animate a camera to the target object's anchor point and optionally change the camera's Angle of View.

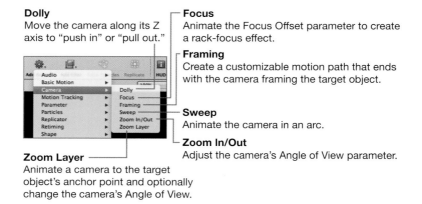

Views

When a camera exists in your 3D project, several view options become available: Camera Menu, 3D View Tools, 3D Compass, and 3D Overlays.

NOTE ▶ If these items do not appear, choose Show 3D Overlays from the View & Overlay Options pop-up menu.

Camera Menu

In the Camera menu, you can choose the view displayed in the Canvas.

NOTE ▶ No matter which view is chosen, exporting the project uses the active cameras according to their time positions and durations in the Timeline.

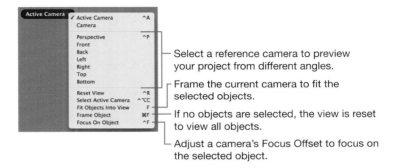

Select a reference camera to preview your project from different angles.

Frame the current camera to fit the selected objects.

If no objects are selected, the view is reset to view all objects.

Adjust a camera's Focus Offset to focus on the selected object.

3D Compass

Using the 3D Compass, you can quickly jump between the active camera and the reference camera views by clicking the desired view.

The view's name appears as you roll over the parts of the compass.

View Layouts

You can create various split-screen views by using the View Layouts pop-up menu.

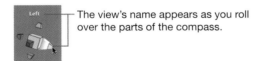

After selecting a split view, click the compass in each view to change the reference view displayed.

The outlined view responds to the
transport controls to play the project.

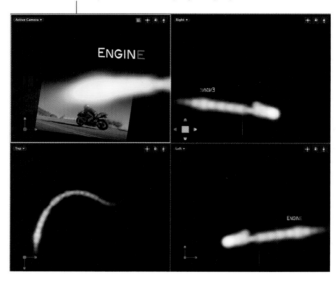

10

Manipulating Objects in 3D

The 3D environment of Motion allows you to manipulate objects or groups along three axes: X, Y, and Z. And like most elements in Motion, if you can manipulate it, you can animate it. Objects and groups may be animated in 3D space using behaviors or keyframes.

2D Layering vs. 3D Positioning

Although you can switch between the 2D and 3D Transform tools to adjust an object or group's position, the group's 2D or 3D status influences the composition. Always remember that in Motion 2D groups (and the objects contained within them) do not intersect with 3D groups or 3D groups' objects.

品 2D 🔒	— Group set to 2D.
▶ 3D 🔒	— Group set to 3D.

In this example, all the groups are set to 2D.

The hierarchical order in the Layers tab determines the compositing order of the groups' objects.

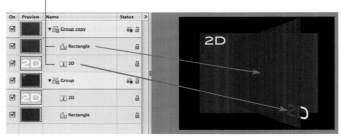

In this example, a mixture of 2D and 3D groups coexist.

The 3D group and its associated objects are composited according to their relative position in 3D space.

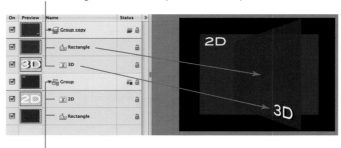

The 2D group and its objects follow their hierarchical order in the Layers tab. The 2D group ignores the positioning of the 3D group.

In this example, all groups are 3D.

The two 3D groups intersect. Their objects are composited according to their positions in 3D space.

Using the 3D Transform Tool in the Canvas

Using the 3D Transform tool in the Canvas, you can scale, position, and rotate an object in 3D space. These adjustments can be keyframed, which allows for precise, custom animation movement.

> **TIP** The 3D Transform tool can also be used with 2D groups, but all objects in the group will occupy the same plane and will not intersect unless switched to 3D.

1   In the Layers tab, click a group's 2D/3D status icon to switch that group to 3D, and then select the group or an object within the group.

2   From the Toolbar, choose the 3D Transform tool, or press the Q key.

3   Adjust the selected layer using the controls in the Canvas.

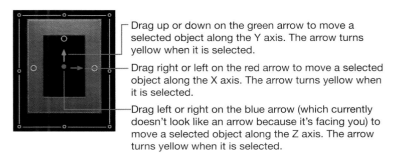

Drag up or down on the green arrow to move a selected object along the Y axis. The arrow turns yellow when it is selected.

Drag right or left on the red arrow to move a selected object along the X axis. The arrow turns yellow when it is selected.

Drag left or right on the blue arrow (which currently doesn't look like an arrow because it's facing you) to move a selected object along the Z axis. The arrow turns yellow when it is selected.

NOTE ▶ Just as with the Select/Transform tool, you can drag an object to freely position it along the X and Y axes.

Drag the X axis rotation handle up or down to rotate the object around the X axis.

Drag the Z axis rotation handle left or right to rotate the object around the Z axis.

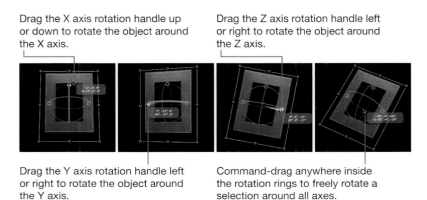

Drag the Y axis rotation handle left or right to rotate the object around the Y axis.

Command-drag anywhere inside the rotation rings to freely rotate a selection around all axes.

NOTE ▶ By default, these adjustments are made according to the object's axes. Motion also allows you to adjust an object based on the world's or the current view's axes. See the next section for information on changing the Adjust Around parameter in the HUD.

Using the 3D Transform Tool in the HUD

When an object or group is selected and the 3D Transform tool is chosen, you can alternatively adjust the layer in the HUD. Drag directly on the Move, Rotate, and Scale controls in the HUD to adjust the layer.

Drag to change the object's position along the Z axis. Drag right to increase the Z value and drag left to decrease the Z value. Command-drag to position an object along the Z axis and scale it at the same time to keep an object at the same perceived size while changing its spatial location.

Drag to change the object's position along the X and Y axes. Drag right to increase the X value and left to decrease it. Drag up to increase the Y value and down to decrease it. Command-drag to constrain movement to the axis that corresponds to the initial drag direction.

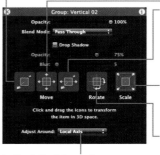

Drag to change the object's position along the X and Z axes. Drag right to increase the X value and left to decrease it. Drag up to increase the Z value and down to decrease it. Command-drag to constrain movement to the axis that corresponds to the initial drag direction.

Drag left or down to decrease the overall scale value of an object. Drag right or up to increase the scale value. Command-drag to constrain scaling to the axis that corresponds to the initial drag direction.

Drag to rotate an object around all axes. Drag up and down to rotate around the X axis. Drag left and right to rotate around the Y axis. Command-drag to constrain the rotation of an object around the Z axis.

In the Adjust Around pop-up menu, you can change the axes used to transform objects in 3D space when using the HUD's and onscreen 3D Transform tools. See the following figures for more information.

TIP ▶ When using the HUD's 3D Transform tools, hold down the Shift key to make larger changes and hold down the Option key to make smaller changes. These keys also work in the Inspector when changing the Position, Rotation, and Scale parameters.

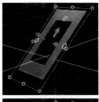

Local axis: Orient the onscreen transform controls to the object's local axes.

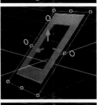

World axis: Orient the transform controls to the World's view. Until a camera is added to a project and repositioned, the World axis will be the same as the View axis with the 3D Transform tool facing the screen.

View axis: Orient the 3D Transform controls to the view space of the current view with the Z axis aligned to the view's line of sight. Until a camera is added to a project and repositioned, the View axis will be the same as the World axis.

3D Behaviors

Some behaviors in Motion have controls that affect an object along three axes. Here are a few examples:

Throw

Click the 3D button and then drag the center arrow to indicate a direction of throw along the X, Y, and Z axes.

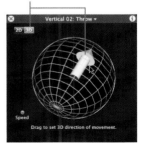

Spin

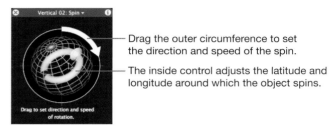

Drag the outer circumference to set the direction and speed of the spin.

The inside control adjusts the latitude and longitude around which the object spins.

Attracted To

Most behaviors do not apply to the Z axis, by default. Select Z to include the Z axis in the behavior's area of influence.

11

Lights, Shadows, and Reflections

Animations in Motion take on a higher level of realism when you move into the 3D environment. This realism is achieved with the use of lights, shadows, and reflections—all items that we take for granted in the world around us, but must be created in Motion.

Motion includes granular controls for lights, shadows, and reflections to add depth and realism to your composition.

Adding a Light

When you want shadow in a project, you begin by adding a light via a menu command or keyboard shortcut.

1   Choose Object > New Light (or press Command-Shift-L). If no 3D group exists in your project, a dialog appears.

2   Click "Switch to 3D" to add a light to the project.

Adjusting Lighting Parameters

As with almost everything in Motion, lights have many parameters that you can modify. These parameters may be keyframed or animated using behaviors. There are two levels of lighting parameters: the parameters of the light itself, and the parameters of the illuminated objects.

Light Parameters

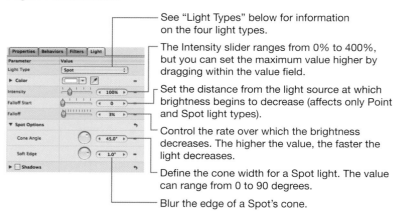

See "Light Types" below for information on the four light types.

The Intensity slider ranges from 0% to 400%, but you can set the maximum value higher by dragging within the value field.

Set the distance from the light source at which brightness begins to decrease (affects only Point and Spot light types).

Control the rate over which the brightness decreases. The higher the value, the faster the light decreases.

Define the cone width for a Spot light. The value can range from 0 to 90 degrees.

Blur the edge of a Spot's cone.

Light Types

Four light types are available in Motion:

Ambient	**Directional**	**Point**	**Spot**
Lights up everything but does not create shadows.	Illuminates only objects that parallel the light's direction. Directional lighting does not decrease with distance.	The default light type, Point is similar to a match or light bulb. Light is emitted in all directions from a single point in space. Point lighting can cast shadows.	Acts like a spotlight that emits light in a controlled, conical pattern. Spot lighting can also cast shadows.

Object Lighting Parameters

In addition to the light's parameters, Motion allows you to control how applicable objects respond to lights in a project. If an object's reaction to light sources is controllable, these parameters will appear in the Properties tab of an object's Inspector.

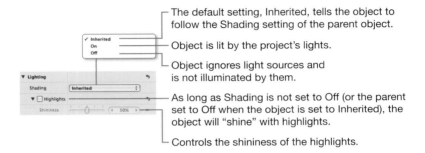

The default setting, Inherited, tells the object to follow the Shading setting of the parent object.

Object is lit by the project's lights.

Object ignores light sources and is not illuminated by them.

As long as Shading is not set to Off (or the parent set to Off when the object is set to Inherited), the object will "shine" with highlights.

Controls the shininess of the highlights.

Disabling Lighting

At times you may want to disable a project's lighting effects to improve real-time playback or to adjust other properties within the project. You can disable the lighting effects by deselecting Lighting in the Render pop-up menu.

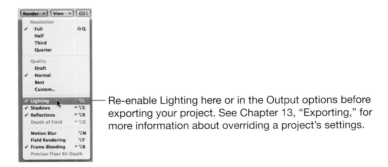

Re-enable Lighting here or in the Output options before exporting your project. See Chapter 13, "Exporting," for more information about overriding a project's settings.

Activating and Adjusting Shadows

Motion includes controls for adding shadows at two levels—on the light and on the 3D objects. To enable objects to cast shadows, your project must have at least one Spot or Point light.

TIP▶ An object can cast a shadow when Lighting is disabled. (See "Disabling Lighting" to disable shading for the project.) These shadows are still controlled by the light's shadow parameters, but do not naturally mix with the object receiving the cast shadows.

Shadow Parameters of a Light

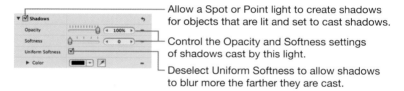

Allow a Spot or Point light to create shadows for objects that are lit and set to cast shadows.

Control the Opacity and Softness settings of shadows cast by this light.

Deselect Uniform Softness to allow shadows to blur more the farther they are cast.

Shadow Parameters of an Object

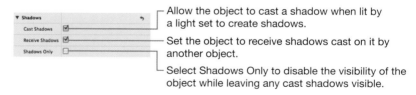

Allow the object to cast a shadow when lit by a light set to create shadows.

Set the object to receive shadows cast on it by another object.

Select Shadows Only to disable the visibility of the object while leaving any cast shadows visible.

NOTE ▶ Cameras and 2D groups do not have shadow controls.

Disabling Shadows

Shadows may be disabled project-wide by deselecting Shadows from the Render pop-up menu. Before outputting your project, remember to re-enable shadows.

Re-enable Shadows here or in the Output options before exporting your project. See Chapter 13, "Exporting," for more information about overriding a project's settings.

Activating and Adjusting Reflections

Objects in Motion may reflect nearby objects. You can adjust the reflection parameters to give an object a natural bit of reflection or a high-gloss shine. There are two levels of reflections: the reflectivity of an object's surface, and whether or not a nearby object is reflected by an object.

Parameters of a Reflector

Reflection parameters are located in the Properties subtab of the Inspector. They affect the reflectivity of an object's surface.

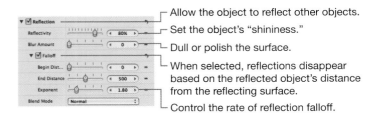

Allow the object to reflect other objects.

Set the object's "shininess."

Dull or polish the surface.

When selected, reflections disappear based on the reflected object's distance from the reflecting surface.

Control the rate of reflection falloff.

Parameter of a Reflected Object

A "shiny" object can have all the reflection it wants, but if nearby objects are not set to cast a reflection, then all you have is a shiny object. The Casts Reflection parameter for nearby objects gives the reflecting object something to reflect. This parameter is also found in the Properties subtab of the Inspector.

The object is available to be reflected.

The object is not reflected by other objects.

The object is rendered invisible, but its reflection is visible.

NOTE ▶ If the group is set to No for Cast Reflections, none of the contained objects will be reflected.

Parameter of the Project

There are two global settings to be aware of when utilizing reflections: Render and Recursive.

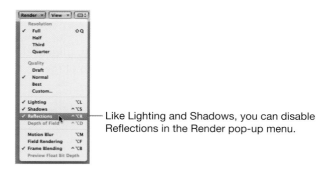

Like Lighting and Shadows, you can disable Reflections in the Render pop-up menu.

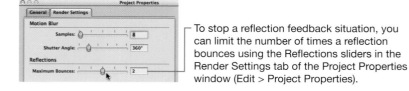

To stop a reflection feedback situation, you can limit the number of times a reflection bounces using the Reflections sliders in the Render Settings tab of the Project Properties window (Edit > Project Properties).

12
Working with Other Applications

This chapter explores the most common workflows you may use when working with Motion and other applications: roundtripping with Final Cut Pro, importing and applying Motion templates in Final Cut Pro, and using Adobe Photoshop and Illustrator documents.

Roundtripping with Final Cut Pro

Final Cut Pro is the application that uses Motion projects most often and for a good reason. Final Cut Pro and Motion are designed to work together to quickly create motion graphics elements for video sequences. Whether adding a title sequence, animating graphical elements, or creating dynamic lower thirds, Motion goes well beyond the graphics capabilities of Final Cut Pro while seamlessly integrating with Final Cut Pro projects.

Three Final Cut Pro parameters should be considered when working with embedded Motion project files.

The first two parameters are in the Render Control tab found under Final Cut Pro > User Preferences.

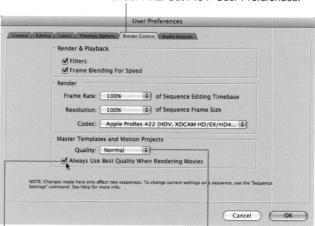

Select the Always Use Best Quality When Rendering Movies checkbox to ensure that final rendered Motion projects will be at their highest quality.

For the best balance of performance and quality, choose Normal Quality for Master Templates and Motion Projects.

The third parameter is found under Sequence > Settings, and in the Video Processing tab.

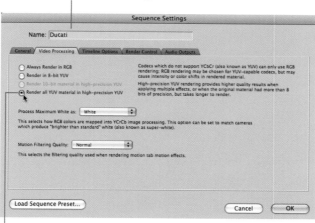

To maintain a Motion project's 16- or 32-bit float rendering mode (when used), the "Render all YUV material in high-precision YUV" checkbox needs to be selected in the Sequence Settings > Video Processing tab. This will force Motion elements used in the sequence to render in 32-bit mode.

Importing and Roundtripping Motion Projects

The most basic integration of Motion into Final Cut Pro is to import and add a native Motion project file to a sequence. Motion projects imported into the Browser are used like any other asset in a project but can be changed in Motion at any time.

1 Import a Motion project file (.motn) into a Final Cut Pro project.

NOTE ► Only the video portion of a Motion project file is imported into Final Cut Pro.

2 From the Browser, edit the .motn clip into the sequence.

3 To change the content of the Motion project, Control-click (or right-click) the Motion project file in the Timeline, and choose "Open in Editor" from the shortcut menu.

4 In Motion, make and save the desired changes to the Motion project.

5 Return to Final Cut Pro to find the .motn file in the Timeline automatically refreshed to reflect the changes.

6 If further changes are needed, repeat steps 3 through 5.

Sending Clips to Motion

You can also create a Motion project file within Final Cut Pro. The new project file may be based on clips in a sequence and may even replace those clips with the new Motion project file.

1 Select one or more sequence clips.

TIP ► Any keyframes set in the Final Cut Pro Motion tab will become part of the new Motion project. Any applied filters will not transfer to Motion (with the exception of the SmoothCam filter, which becomes the Stabilize behavior in Motion).

2 Control-click the selected content and choose Send To > Motion Project from the shortcut menu.

3 Name the new Motion project, choose a save location, and choose any other options you desire.

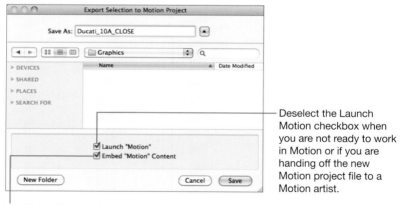

Deselect the Launch Motion checkbox when you are not ready to work in Motion or if you are handing off the new Motion project file to a Motion artist.

The Embed Motion Content checkbox is selected by default. This function replaces the selected clip with the new Motion project file. Deselect this checkbox if the clips are intended for use as a reference background on which to build graphics.

4 In Motion, build and save the Motion project.

NOTE ► If the original clip from Final Cut Pro was sent for reference only, be sure to disable that layer before saving.

5 Return to Final Cut Pro. An embedded project will automatically replace the selected clip(s) in the Final Cut Pro sequence.

TIP ▶ If you deselected the Embed Motion Content checkbox in step 3, you will need to manually import the Motion project file into the Browser and edit the project into the sequence.

Sending Sequences to Motion

Rather than sending a clip or two, Final Cut Pro allows you to create a new Motion project file from a sequence.

1 Select the sequence in the Browser.

2 Control-click the sequence and choose Send To > Motion Project from the shortcut menu.

3 Name the new Motion project and choose a save location.

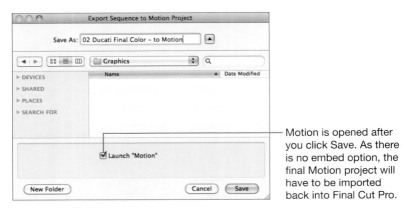

Motion is opened after you click Save. As there is no embed option, the final Motion project will have to be imported back into Final Cut Pro.

4   In Motion, build and save the Motion project.

5   Return to Final Cut Pro and import the saved Motion project
    into the Final Cut Pro project.

Using Motion Templates in Final Cut Pro

Applying and working with templates in Final Cut Pro is slightly different from importing a Motion project and adding it to a sequence.
Motion templates can be updated dynamically in Final Cut Pro,
which allows you to change the media used in drop zones and the
text used in the template.

1   In a Final Cut Pro sequence, cue the playhead to the location
    where you want to add the master template.

2   In Final Cut Pro, choose Sequence > Add Master Template.

3   In the Master Template Browser, select the Master Template.

Choose a template by first selecting the appropriate theme and
then choosing the desired master template from that theme.

4   At the lower right of the Master Template Browser, choose a
    Superimpose, Overwrite, or Insert edit.

NOTE ▶ These edit options are available only if the Timeline was active when you performed step 2.

5   Use the controls in the Viewer to add media to drop zones and to change text.

Drag media from the Browser to the Controls tab's image wells to add stills or movies to the template's drop zones.

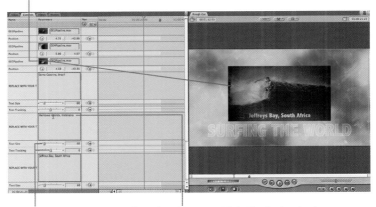

Drag the sliders to adjust the   Enter text into the text entry boxes
text size or tracking settings.   to replace the template's text areas.

NOTE ▶ The controls for the template should automatically load into the Viewer. If not, double-click the template in the sequence.

Working with Adobe Photoshop Documents

Adobe Photoshop is the standard design tool for many graphics professionals. Luckily, Motion has great support for layered Photoshop documents and even retains the opacity and the majority of blending modes that are applied to the image.

1   In the File Browser of Motion, select a .psd file.

2   Drag the file to the Canvas, Layers tab, or Timeline.

3   Wait for the drop menu to appear and choose whether to import a merged version of the .psd file, all layers from the .psd file, or an individual layer.

The drop menu as it appears in the Canvas.

4   Apply behaviors and/or filters, and animate them as you would any other object in Motion.

Working with Adobe Illustrator Documents

Adobe Illustrator files can be imported into Motion. To ensure compatibility, make sure the Create PDF Compatible File checkbox is selected when saving an Illustrator file.

1   Import the Adobe Illustrator document into the Motion project.

2   In the Media tab of the Project pane, select the Illustrator file that was imported into the project.

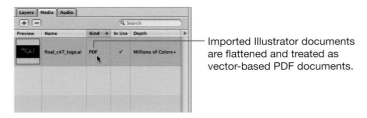

Imported Illustrator documents are flattened and treated as vector-based PDF documents.

3   Press F4 to go to the Media tab of the Inspector.

4   Deselect the Fixed Resolution checkbox.

By default, the Fixed Resolution option is selected when importing Illustrator documents, and the resolution will be based on the original file's resolution. By deselecting this option, the vector file can be scaled to any size.

13

Exporting

When you are satisfied with your composition, Motion provides two output methods: Export and Share. These two methods include both simple and advanced export options.

Using File > Export

The Export command allows you to apply export presets or customize the output settings. Not only will you select which video codec to use (and audio codec, when applicable), but you'll also be able to activate/deactivate specific project settings such as depth of field, shadows, and reflections.

1   Choose File > Export.

2   Type a name for the output file in the Save As field, and from the Where pop-up menu choose a destination.

3   Select the remaining parameters as desired.

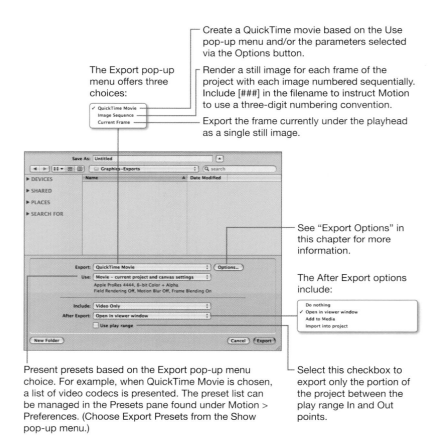

Create a QuickTime movie based on the Use pop-up menu and/or the parameters selected via the Options button.

The Export pop-up menu offers three choices:

Render a still image for each frame of the project with each image numbered sequentially. Include [###] in the filename to instruct Motion to use a three-digit numbering convention.

Export the frame currently under the playhead as a single still image.

See "Export Options" in this chapter for more information.

The After Export options include:

Present presets based on the Export pop-up menu choice. For example, when QuickTime Movie is chosen, a list of video codecs is presented. The preset list can be managed in the Presets pane found under Motion > Preferences. (Choose Export Presets from the Show pop-up menu.)

Select this checkbox to export only the portion of the project between the play range In and Out points.

Export Options

When a preset doesn't meet your needs or if advanced options are necessary, you can click the Options button to go deeper into the output settings. You have two tabs in the Export Options window when exporting a QuickTime movie: Video/Audio and Output.

Choose from the same
options as in the Export
pop-up menu in the Export
dialog (previous figure).

Choose a codec.

Click the Advanced button
to access the QuickTime
Compression Settings
window, in which you can
set additional parameters
such as frame rate and
data rate, depending on
the chosen codec.

Access the QuickTime
Sound Settings window.

Click Save As to create a
new preset based on
these settings.

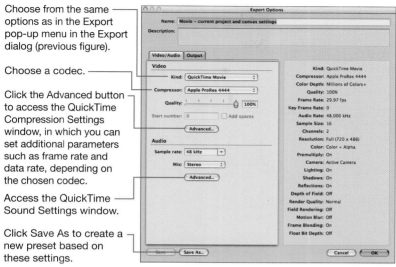

Selected by default,
deselect this checkbox,
as shown here, to
customize the export
settings.

Choose a preset
Resolution (Full, Half,
Third, Quarter, or a
preset frame size) or
choose Custom and use
the frame size fields to
specify the custom size.

Activate/deactivate
project and rendering
settings to customize
the output.

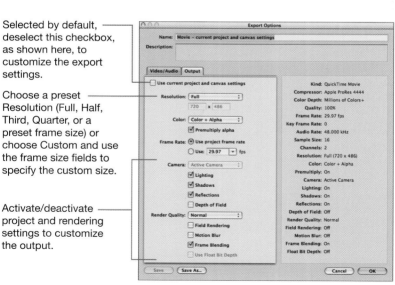

Using File > Share

The Share command in Motion is similar to the Share features of Final Cut Pro. This command provides quick access to common export options and background processing.

Select to export only the marked play range of the project.

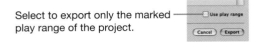

The Output drawer allows access to the export options for overriding the current project and Canvas settings

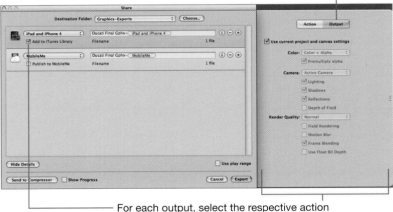

For each output, select the respective action checkbox to open the Action/Output drawer.

Keyboard Shortcuts

This appendix lists the most commonly used Motion commands, organized by function. Refer to the *Motion User Manual* for a full list of keyboard shortcuts.

Interface

Function	Shortcut	Action
Standard	Control-U	Set the interface to the Standard window layout.
File Browser	Command-1	Bring the File Browser tab of the Utility window to the front.
Library	Command-2	Bring the Library tab of the Utility window to the front.
Inspector	Command-3	Bring the Inspector tab of the Utility window to the front.
Layers	Command-4	Bring the Layers tab of the Project pane to the front.

Function	Shortcut	Action
Media	Command-5	Bring the Media tab of the Project pane to the front.
Audio	Command-6	Bring the Audio tab of the Project pane to the front.
Timeline	Command-7	Bring the Timeline tab of the Timing pane to the front.
Keyframe Editor	Command-8	Bring the Keyframe Editor tab of the Timing pane to the front.
Audio Editor	Command-9	Bring the Audio Editor tab of the Timing pane to the front.
Properties	F1	Bring the Properties subtab of the Inspector to the front.
Behaviors	F2	Bring the Behaviors subtab of the Inspector to the front.
Filters	F3	Bring the Filters subtab of the Inspector to the front.
Object	F4	Bring the Object subtab of the Inspector to the front. The Object tab changes depending on the object type. (For example, it becomes the Text tab when a text object is selected.)

Function	Shortcut	Action
Project pane	F5	Show/Hide the Project pane within the Canvas window.
Timing pane	F6	Show/Hide the Timing pane within the Canvas window.
HUD	F7	Show/Hide the heads-up display.
Cycle HUD	D	Cycle the HUD through the selected object's Properties parameters, and/or Object parameters, plus the parameters of any applied filters and behaviors.
Full Screen mode	F8	Show/Hide the Canvas area as full screen. Overlays may be shown or hidden.
Cycle project windows	Command-`	Display the next open project's Canvas window.

View Tools

Function	Shortcut	Action
Select/ Transform	Shift-S	Select an object in the Canvas or modify an object using its transform handles in the Canvas. Alternatively, press the Tab key to cycle through the selection tools.
Adjust Anchor Point	Tab	Modify the object's anchor point.
Adjust Shear	Tab	Shear the side of an object.
Adjust Drop Shadow	Tab	Modify the drop shadow of an object.
Adjust Four Corner	Tab	Modify the corner of an object.
Adjust Crop	Tab	Modify the crop of an object.
Adjust Control Points	Tab	Modify a shape's control points.
Adjust Glyph	Tab	Transform the position/orientation of glyphs.
Select Transform	S	Transform an object in the Canvas. Alternatively, press the Tab key to cycle through the selection tools.
Adjust 3D Transform	Q	Adjust the position or rotation of an object along the X, Y, and Z axes.

Function	Shortcut	Action
Pan	H	Adjust the Canvas view along the X and Y axes. Alternatively, hold down the Spacebar while dragging in the Canvas.
Zoom	Z	Zoom the Canvas view.

Create Tools

Function	Shortcut	Action
Rectangle	R	Shift-drag to maintain aspect ratio. Option-drag to scale from the center of the object.
Circle	C	Shift-drag to maintain aspect ratio. Option-drag to scale from the center of the object.
Bezier	B	Click the first point to close the shape. Double-click the last point to create an open shape.
B-Spline	B	Click the first point to close the shape. Double-click the last point to create an open shape.
Paint Stroke	P	Drag with this tool to create a continuous stroke.
Text	T	After entering text, press Esc to exit text entry.

Mask Tools

Function	Shortcut	Action
Rectangle Mask	Option-R	Create a mask based on a rectangular shape.
Circle Mask	Option-C	Create a mask based on a circular shape.
Freehand Mask	Option-P	Create a mask based on a continuous dragging motion.
Bezier Mask	Option-B	Click the first point to close the mask's shape. Double-click the last point to create an open mask shape.
B-Spline Mask	Option-B	Click the first point to close the mask's shape. Double-click the last point to create an open mask shape.
Add Image Mask	Command-Shift-M	Create a mask from the content (channels) of an object.

Camera and Effects Icons

Function	Shortcut	Action
New Camera	Command-Option-C	Add a camera to the project.
Make Particles	E	Create a particle system based on the selected object.
Replicate	L	Create a replicator pattern based on the selected object.

Canvas

Function	Shortcut	Action
Play	Spacebar	Play/Pause
Fit to Window	Shift-Z	Scale the Canvas area to fill the Canvas window.
Zoom Level 100%	Option-Z	Set the Canvas zoom to 100%.
Show Overlays	Command-/	Show/Hide the overlays (rulers, guides, handles, and so on) in the Canvas.
Show 3D Overlays	Command-Option-/	Show/Hide the 3D overlays (3D Grid, Compass, Inset View, and so on).

Function	Shortcut	Action
Show Full View Area	Shift-V	Show/Hide objects outside the viewable Canvas area.
Reset View	Control-R	Reset the current view.
Focus on Object	Control-F	Adjust the camera's focus to the selected object.
Nudge	Command-Arrow keys	Move the selected object by one pixel in the direction of the arrow key used.

Timing

Function	Shortcut	Action
Mark Play Range In	Command-Option-I	Set the play range In point at the playhead's position in the mini-Timeline or Timing pane.
Mark Play Range Out	Command-Option-O	Set the play range Out point at the playhead's position in the mini-Timeline or Timing pane.
Reset Play Range	Option-X	Clear the play range In and Out points.
Move In Point	Shift-{	Move the selected item to align its In point to the playhead.
Move Out Point	Shift-}	Move the selected item to align its Out point to the playhead.

Function	Shortcut	Action
Nudge Forward	Command-Right Arrow	Move the selected object one frame to the right.
Nudge Backward	Command-Left Arrow	Move the selected object one frame to the left.
Marker	M	Add a marker at the playhead.
Add Keyframe	Control-K	Add a keyframe to the selected object (to the last modified parameter).

Project

Function	Shortcut	Action
Group Selected	Command-Shift-G	Group the selected objects into a new group.
Deactivate Object	Command-T	Activate/Deactivate the selected object.
Solo	Control-S	Solo the selected track.
Clone	K	Clone the selected layer.

Index

Symbols and Numbers

2D groups
  2D layering vs. 3D positioning, 113–114
  adding camera to project, 106
  designating, 14
  shadow controls not working with, 122
3D behaviors, 117–118
3D Compass, camera view, 111
3D groups
  3D positioning vs. 2D layering, 113–114
  adding camera to project, 106
  designating, 14
  positioning camera, 107–109
3D Transform tool (Q key), 114–117
3D view tools, camera, 109

A

Add Behavior button, 13, 32
Add Filter button, 13
Add, Mask Blend Mode, 41
Adjust 3D Transform tool, 29, 107–109
Adjust Anchor Point tool, 11, 141
Adjust Glyph tool, 29–30
Adobe Illustrator documents, 132–133
Adobe Photoshop documents, 131–132
Advanced pane, Shape tab, 44–45

Advanced Quality, Canvas display, 9
After Exports options, Export command, 136–137
alpha channels
  particle cell parameters, 53
  replicator cell parameters, 61
Ambient light, 120
anchor points
  adding camera behaviors, 110
  Adjust Anchor Point tool, 11, 142
  in Canvas window, 8
  differentiating camera types by, 107
  replicators and, 60
Animation menu
  applying extrapolation to keyframes, 83–84
  converting behaviors to keyframes, 86
  keyframing filters in, 99
  keyframing parameters in, 80
  manually creating keyframes in, 77–78
  Properties tab in Inspector, 4
  setting interpolation in, 18
  taking curve snapshots in, 83
Apply button, 3
Apply To parameter, of parameter behaviors, 93
Audio parameter behavior, 94
audio, Show/Hide Layers in Timeline, 17
Audio tab (Command-6), 16–17

axes
    3D behaviors, 117–118
    manipulating objects in 3D
        along, 113
    using 3D Transform tool in
        Canvas, 115
    using 3D Transform tool in
        HUD, 116–117

B

B-Spline Mask tool (Option-B), 12,
    40, 143
B-Spline tool (B)
    Bezier curves vs. shapes of, 38
    as Create tool, 12
    escaping incomplete shape, 38
    modifying closed shape, 39
Bad Film filter, 104
Basic Motion behavior, replicators, 64
behaviors
    3D, 117–118
    applying, 13, 87–88
    camera, 110
    converting to keyframes, 86
    examples of, 90–92
    modifying, 89–90
    overview of, 87
    parameter, 92–96
    particle, 56
    replicator, 64–66
    showing/hiding/disabling in
        Layers tab, 14
    showing/hiding in
        Timeline tab, 17
    text, 32–34
    timing/duration of. see timelines
Behaviors tab (F2)
    modifying behaviors, 89

modifying parameter
    behaviors, 93–95
    project behaviors listed in, 4–5
Bezier Mask tool (Option-B), 12,
    40–41, 144
Bezier tool (B)
    B-spline shapes vs. curves of, 38
    as Create tool, 12
    creating custom shapes with,
        36–38
    modifying closed shapes with, 39
    placing text on path with, 28
blur filters, camera, 103, 106
Box tool, 18, 81
Brightness, light parameters, 120
Brush Types, Shape tab, 39

C

Camera and Effects icons, 12–13, 145
cameras
    adding, 13, 105–106
    adding multiple, 106
    behaviors, 110
    modifying, 106–107
    positioning, 107–109
    shadow controls lacking on, 122
    types of, 107
    view options, 110–112
Canvas
    3D Transform tool in, 114–115
    applying filters in, 98–99
    in Canvas window, 6–8
    creating particle system in, 50–51
    creating replicators in, 58–59
    keyboard shortcuts, 145-146
    overview of, 6–8
Canvas window
    Canvas, 6–8
    defined, 6

mini-Timeline, 9–10
showing/hiding Project/Timing
    panes of, 13
Status Bar, 8
View Options, 8–9
Casts Reflection parameter, 123–124
categories
    behaviors, 87
    filters, 97
channels, setting visibility, 9
Circle tool, 35–36
Clone layers, creating, 16
color
    modifying closed shapes, 39
    modifying filters, 99
    modifying paint strokes, 44
    setting particle cell parameters,
        53–54
    setting replicator cell
        parameters, 60–62
    Shape tab options, 39
Command-2. see Library tab
    (Command-2)
Command-4. see Layers tab
    (Command-4)
Command-5 (Media tab), 16
Command-7. see Timeline tab
    (Command-7)
Command-8. see Keyframe Editor
    (Command-8)
Command-9 (Audio Editor),
    18–19, 140
Command-D (duplicating layer), 16
Command Editor, 22
Command-Option-I (Play Range
    In Point), 10
Command-Option-O (Play Range
    Out Point), 10
Command-Shift-L (New Light), 119

commands. see keyboard shortcuts
Composite import, 68–69, 72
cone width setting, Spot light, 120
Control-click, 7
control points
    creating custom shapes, 36–38
    placing text on path, 28
Convert to Keyframes, 86
copy filters, 100
Crawl command, Layout tab, 27
Create tools
    keyboard shortcuts, 143
    in Toolbar, 11–12
credits, creating scrolling, 32–34
Crop option, filters, 102
Current Frame, Export menu, 136
curve snapshots, Keyframe Editor,
    18, 82–83
curves, Keyframe Editor settings, 18

D

Defocus blur filter, 106
Depth of Field parameters, camera,
    106–107
destination object
    applying behaviors to, 88
    applying filters to, 98–99
directional light, 120
Disclosure triangle, Properties tab, 4
display mode, for objects in Canvas, 9
documents
    working with Adobe
        Photoshop, 131–132
    working with Illustrator,
        132–133
duplicate behaviors, 89
duplicate layers, 16
duration
    behavior, 89–90
    filter, 101

E

Earthquake filter, 103
Edit Marker dialog, 76
Edit tool, keyframes, 18
editing
    keyframes. see Keyframe Editor
        (Command-8)
    keyframes in Timeline, 85
    Motion templates in Final Cut
        Pro, 130–131
Embed Motion Content checkbox,
    128–129
emitters, particle system
    defined, 49
    particle cell parameters, 52–54
    shapes, 55–56
Escape key, from text entry mode, 24
Exchange import option, Timeline, 72
Export command, 135–137
exporting
    using File > Export, 135–137
    using File > Share, 138
extrapolation, Keyframe Editor,
    83–84

F

F3 (Filters tab), Inspector, 5
F4 (Object tab), 3–6
F5. see Project pane (F5)
F6. see Timing pane (F6)
fade in/out, camera, 106
File Browser tab (Command-1), 2
File > Export, exporting, 135–137
File > Share, exporting, 138
File text generator, 30
filters
    adjusting timing/duration of.
        see timelines
    applying, 13, 98–99
    examples of, 102–104
    modifying, 99–102

    overview of, 97
    for particle systems, 56
    for replicators, 64–66
    selecting camera blur, 106
    showing/hiding/disabling in
        Layers tab, 14
    showing/hiding in
        Timeline tab, 17
Filters tab (F3), Inspector, 5
Final Cut Pro
    importing and roundtripping
        Motion projects, 127
    overview of, 125–126
    sending clips to Motion, 127–129
    sending sequences to Motion,
        129–130
    using Motion templates with,
        130–131
Final Cut Pro Set tool, 22
Fixed Resolution option,
    Illustrator, 133
focus, camera, 106
font families, modifying text, 24
Format pane, modifying text, 24
Framing camera, 107
Freehand Mask tool, 40–41

G

Gaussian Blur filter, camera, 103, 106
generators, text, 30–31
glyphs, text, 29–30, 34
gradient editor
    modifying closed shapes, 39
    modifying paint strokes, 44
    setting particle cell parameters,
        53–54
    setting replicator cell
        parameters, 62
groups
    applying filters to, 97
    applying mask tools to text in, 41

consolidating layers into, 13–14
using 3D Transform tool with
2D, 114–115
grunging video, with Bad Film
filter, 104
guides, Canvas, 9

H

Highlights, lighting parameters, 121
HUD (Heads-Up Display), F7
3D Transform tool in, 116–117
modifying behaviors in, 89–90
modifying cameras in, 106–107
modifying filters in, 99–100
modifying masks in, 41
modifying paint strokes in, 44
modifying particle systems in, 51
modifying replicators in, 59
modifying text in, 29
overview of, 19
positioning camera in, 108
showing/hiding, 13

I

Illustrator documents, 132–133
image masks, 41–42
Image Sequence, Export menu, 136
Import button, File Browser, 2
importing
Adobe Illustrator files, 132–133
Motion project into
Final Cut Pro, 127
objects with File Browser, 2
referencing file at its current
location when, 2
Timeline options, 72
In points
in mini-Timeline, 69–70
in Timeline, 72–74
Inherited, lighting parameters, 121

Insert import option, Timeline, 72
Inspector tab (Command-3)
applying behaviors, 87–88
Behaviors tab in, 4–5
defined, 3
Filters tab in, 5
modifying behaviors in, 89–90
modifying cameras in, 106–107
modifying filters in, 99–102
modifying particle systems in,
51–56
modifying replicators in, 59–61
modifying text in, 24–28
Object tab in, 4–5
Properties tab in, 4
setting keyframes manually in,
77–78
Utility window in, 3–6
Intensity slider, light parameters, 120
Interface
keyboard shortcuts, 139–141
Toolbar buttons, 13
interpolation, 18, 81–82
Intersect, Mask Blend Mode, 41

J

Jitter, modifying paint stroke, 44
Joint option, Shape tab, 39

K

kerning, modifying text, 24
keyboard shortcuts
Camera and Effects icons, 145
Canvas, 145-146
Create tools, 143
customizing, 22
Interface, 139–141
Mask tools, 144
Project, 147
Timing, 146-147
View tools, 11, 142-143

Keyframe Editor (Command-8)
    creating keyframes in, 80–81
    defined, 80
    editing keyframes in, 81
    mini-curve editor in, 84–85
    setting extrapolation in, 83–84
    setting interpolation in, 81–82
    taking curve snapshots, 82–83
    in Timing pane, 18
keyframes
    converting behaviors to, 86
    creating with Record
        Animation, 79–80
    for filters, 99
    Keyframe Editor. see Keyframe
        Editor (Command-8)
    modifying in Timeline, 85
    overview of, 77
    sending clips to Motion from
        Final Cut Pro, 128
    setting manually, 77–78
    showing/hiding in
        Timeline tab, 17
    thinning options, 79

L
layers
    adjusting row heights, 17
    showing/hiding in
        Timeline tab, 17
Layers tab (Command-4)
    applying behaviors, 87–88
    applying filters, 98–99
    creating particle system, 50–51
    creating replicator, 58–59
    modifying text, 24
    in Project pane, 13–16
Layout pane, modifying text, 26–28
Library tab (Command-2)
    finding text generators in, 30–31
    overview of, 3

selecting filter in, 98
using preset particle systems in,
    49–50
using preset replicators in, 57–58
life cycles, particle system, 49, 53–54
lighting
    activating and adjusting
        reflections, 123–124
    activating and adjusting
        shadows, 122–123
    adding to project, 119
    adjusting parameters for, 120–121
    disabling, 121
    types of, 120
Line tool, 35–36
Linear shape, 39
Link parameter behavior, 95
local axis, 3D Transform tool
    in HUD, 117
locking, 6, 14
looping clips, in mini-Timeline, 70–71

M
Make Particles button, 13
markers, 76
Mask tools, 12, 143
masks
    adding image to, 41–43
    creating, 40–41
    modifying, 41
    modifying control points, 45
    showing/hiding/disabling in
        Layers tab, 14
    showing/hiding in
        Timeline tab, 17
master template, 130–131
Match Move behavior, 92
Media tab (Command-5), 16
mini-curve editor, 84–85
mini-Timeline
    adding multiple objects to, 68–69

adding single objects to, 68
adjusting timing/duration of
   behaviors in, 89–90
adjusting timing/duration of
   filters in, 101
in Canvas window, 7, 9–10
defined, 67
looping clips in, 70–71
moving objects in, 69
project and object markers in, 76
retiming clips in, 70
trimming objects in, 69–70
mix level, audio files, 17
Motion basics
   Canvas window, 6–10
   Heads-Up Display, 19
   overview of, 1
   Project pane, 13–17
   properties and preferences,
      19–22
   Timing pane, 17–19
   Toolbar, 10–13
   Utility window, 2–6
Move behavior, 87, 89
mute, Audio tab, 17

N

Negate behavior, 87
New Camera icon, 13, 105–106
New folder, File Browser, 2
New Light (Command-Shift-L), 119
Nudge behavior, 87
Numbers text generator, 31

O

object markers, 76
Object tab (F4), 3–6
objects
   adjusting timing/duration of.
      see timelines

animating with behaviors. see
   behaviors
applying filters to. see filters
parameters of reflected, 123–124
shadow parameters of, 122
opacity
   modifying closed shape, 39
   modifying paint stroke, 44
   setting particle cell parameters, 53
   setting replicator cell
      parameters, 60–62
Option key, 36, 116
Option-X, 10
Oscillate Shape behavior, 46
Out points
   in mini-Timeline, 69–70
   in Timeline, 72–74
Output, Export Options, 136–137
Output, Share command, 138
overlays, 9
Overwrite import option, Timeline, 72

P

Paint Stroke tool, 43–45
parameter behaviors
   applying, 92–93
   applying to filters, 99
   applying to replicators, 64
   defined, 87
parameters
   choosing in Keyframe Editor, 18
   example of filter, 103–104
   Final Cut Pro, 125–126
   lighting, 120–121
   modifying filter, 99–102
   modifying text, 27–28
   particle cell, 52–54
   reflection, 123
   replicator cell, 60–62
   tweaking in Properties tab, 4

Particle Emitters, 49–50
particle systems
  behaviors and filters for, 56
  creating, 50–51
  creating from selected layer, 13
  defined, 49
  emitter shapes, 55–56
  modifying, 51–52
  parameters of particle cell, 52–54
  using preset, 49–50
path, placing text on, 27–28
Photoshop documents, working
  with, 131–132
Play Range In Point (Command-
  Option-I), 10
Play Range Out Point (Command-
  Option-O), 10
playback, recording keyframes
  during, 79–80
playhead
  moving object in Timeline to,
    72–73
  setting keyframes manually
    with, 77–78
  slipping clips in Timeline, 74
  splitting clips in Timeline, 73
Point light, 120
point size, text, 24
positioning
  2D layering vs. 3D, 113–114
  cameras, 107–109
  using 3D Transform tool,
    114–117
preferences, setting, 8, 21
presets
  applying style to text objects, 26
  choosing project, 20
  Export command, 135–136
  using particle system, 49–50
  using replicator, 57–58
Preview area, File Browser, 2
project markers, 76

Project pane (F5)
  Audio tab, 16–17
  defined, 13
  keyboard shortcuts, 146
  Layers tab, 13–16
  location of, 7
  Media tab, 16
  showing/hiding in Canvas
    window, 6, 13
project presets, 20
Project Properties window, Render
  Settings tab, 124
properties, setting project, 20
Properties tab (F1), Inspector, 4
.psd files, 131–132

Q

QuickTime movie, Export
  command, 136–137

R

Randomize Shape behavior, 46
Record Animation button, 10, 79–80
Rectangle or Circle Mask tool, 40
Rectangle tool, 35–36
Recursive setting, reflections, 124
Reduce Keyframes, Animation
  menu, 85
reflections, 123–124
regions, creating time, 74–75
regular behaviors. see behaviors
render options
  in Final Cut Pro, 126
  setting Canvas, 9
  working with reflections, 124
Replace, Mask Blend Mode, 41
Replicate button, 13
replicators
  behaviors and filters for, 64–66
  creating, 58–59
  defined, 57

modifying, 59
replicator cell parameters, 60–62
shapes of, 63–64
using preset, 57–58
Reset button, Properties tab, 4
resolution, in Canvas, 9
Retiming behaviors, 91
retiming clips, in mini-Timeline, 70
ripple deletes (Shift-Delete), 75
rotation
    modifying text in Inspector, 24
    Shift-[/ Shift-] moving
        selections in playhead, 8
    using 3D Transform tool,
        114–117
roundtripping. see Final Cut Pro

S

scale
    in Canvas window, 8
    modifying text in Inspector, 24
    in particle systems, 56
    using 3D Transform tool,
        114–117
Scroll command, Layout tab, 27
Scroll Text behavior, 32
Select/Transform tool
    adjusting timing and duration
        of behaviors, 90
    adjusting timing and duration
        of filters, 101
    creating text, 24
Sequence Paint behavior, 47
Sequence Replicator behavior, 64–66
Sequence Text behavior, 32–33
sequences, sending to Motion from
    Final Cut Pro, 129–130
Sequential import, 68–69, 72
Set Speed behavior, 91
shadows
    activating and adjusting, 122

disabling and re-enabling,
    122–123
lighting for, 119
lighting parameters for, 120–121
Shape tab, Inspector, 38–40, 44–45
shapes
    behaviors for, 46–48
    converting to paint strokes, 43–45
    creating masks, 40–43
    custom, 36–38
    emitter, 55–56
    modifying closed, 38–39
    modifying control points, 45
    replicator, 63–64
    simple, 35–36
Share command, exporting, 138
Shift-[/ Shift-] moving selections in
    playhead, 73
Shift-Delete (ripple delete), 75
Shift key, 36, 116
Show/Hide Keyframes button, 85
Simulation behavior, replicators, 64
Sketch tool, 18, 80
slipping clips, Timeline, 74
snapping
    enabling/disabling in Keyframe
        Editor, 18
    turning off when moving
        clips, 69
snapshots, curve, 82–83
Solo, in Audio tab, 17
Spin Over Life behavior, 56
splitting clips, 73
Spot light, 120
Stabilize behavior, 92
Stack, File Browser, 2
Status bar, 7, 8
Stroke pane, Shape tab, 44–45
Style pane, 25–26
Subtract, Mask Blend Mode, 41

T

Tab key, Toolbar, 11
Take/Show Curve Snapshot button,
    Keyframe Editor, 82–83
templates, using in Final Cut Pro,
    130–131
text
    behaviors, 32–34
    creating, 23–24
    generators, 30–31
    modifying in HUD, 29
    modifying in Inspector tab,
        24–28
    overview of, 23
    using Adjust Glyph tool, 29–30
Text subtab, Inspector, 24
Text tool, 23–24
3D behaviors, 117–118
3D Compass, camera view, 111
3D groups
    3D positioning vs. 2D layering,
        113–114
    adding camera to project, 106
    designating, 14
    positioning camera, 107–109
3D Transform tool (Q key), 114–117
3D view tools, camera, 109
Time Date text generator, 31
time regions, 74–75
Timecode text generator, 31
Timeline tab (Command-7)
    adding objects to, 71–72
    adjusting timing and duration
        of behaviors, 89–90
    adjusting timing and duration
        of filters, 101
    creating time regions in, 74–75
    defined, 67
    mini-Timeline functions in, 67
    modifying keyframes in, 85

moving object to playhead in,
    72–73
slipping clips in, 74
splitting clips in, 73
in Timing pane, 17
timelines
    mini-Timeline, 67–71
    overview of, 67
    Timeline tab, 71–75
    working with markers, 76
Timing pane (F6)
    Audio Editor tab, 18–19
    keyboard shortcuts, 145–146
    Keyframe Editor tab, 18
    location of, 7
    showing/hiding in Canvas
        window, 6, 13
    Timeline tab, 17
tinting, 53, 61
Title Safe area, 24
Toolbar
    adding camera to project from,
        105–106
    Camera and Effects buttons,
        12–13
    Create tools, 11–12
    Interface buttons, 13
    location of, 7
    Mask tools, 12, 40
    overview of, 10
    View tools, 11
Track Points behavior, 47
Tracking behavior, 91–92
tracking, modifying text, 24
Transform controls, 107–109
Transform Glyph attribute, Adjust
    Glyph tool, 29
Transform tool, 3D
    in Canvas, 114–115
    in HUD, 116–117

trimming objects, in mini-Timeline,
69–70
2D groups
2D layering vs. 3D positioning,
113–114
adding camera to project, 106
designating, 14
shadow controls not working
with, 122

U

Unstabilize behavior, 92
user interface, buttons, 13
User Preferences, Final Cut Pro
parameters, 126
Utility window, 2–6

V

Video/Audio, Export Options,
136–137
Video Processing tab, Final Cut Pro
parameters, 126
view axis, 3D Transform tool in
HUD, 117
View Layouts menu, 9, 112–113
View options, Canvas, 7–9
View tools, 11, 141–142
Viewer, using templates in
Final Cut Pro, 131
Viewpoint camera, 107
views
camera options, 105, 110–111
modifying camera, 106–107
positioning camera, 107–109

W

Walk Camera tool, 109
world axis, 3D Transform tool in
HUD, 117
Wriggle parameter behavior, 95–96
Wriggle shape behavior, 48
Write On behavior, 48

Z

zoom, 9, 17